Flying in Father's Slipstream
Leaves from our Flying Logbooks 1929-2010

Air Commodore Harry Eeles (CB, CBE) and his son **Group Captain Tom Eeles** (BA, FRAeS) were both pilots in the Royal Air Force from 1929 to 2010. Their combined flying experience covers a period of eighty years, ranging from the early days of a young air force equipped with rudimentary biplanes to flying the complex aircraft of the twenty first century. This book uses entries from both pilot's military flying logbooks to describe the personal, technical details and the broader circumstances of each flight, also covering the general background of the time, both within the Royal Air Force and the wider world.

Flying in Father's Slipstream

Leaves from our Flying Logbooks 1929-2010

Tom Eeles

Arena Books

Copyright © Tom Eeles, 2018

The right of Tom Eeles to be identified as author of this book has been asserted in accordance with the Copyright, Designs and Patents Act 1988.

First published in 2018 by Arena Books

Arena Books
6 Southgate Green
Bury St. Edmunds
IP33 2BL

www.arenabooks.co.uk

Distributed in America by Ingram International, One Ingram Blvd., PO Box 3006, La Vergne, TN 37086-1985, USA.

All rights reserved. Except for the quotation of short passages for the purposes of criticism and review, no part of this publication may be reproduced, stored in a retrieval system, or transmitted, in any form or by any means, electronic, mechanical, photocopying, recording or otherwise, without the prior permission of the publisher. All characters portrayed are fictitious and any resemblance to real persons, living or dead, is purely coincidental.

Tom Eeles
Flying in Father's Slipstream Leaves from our flying Logbooks 1929-2010

British Library cataloguing in Publication Data. A Catalogue record for this book is available from the British Library.

ISBN-13 978-1-911593-22-5

BIC classifications:- BGA, BGH, BTM, HBW, HBWS, HBLW.

Printed and bound by Lightning Source UK

Cover design
By Jason Anscomb

Typeset in
Times New Roman

CONTENTS

Foreword		9
Preface		11
Chapters -		
One.	In the Beginning, Cranwell 1929	13
Two.	Cranwell in the 1960s	20
Three.	The Best Flying Club in the World	28
Four.	Nearly the Best Flying Club in the Far East	32
Five.	Hard Work in the Desert	42
Six.	The Barren Rocks of Aden	47
Seven.	An Instructional Interlude	53
Eight.	Instructing Thirty-Two Years Later	58
Nine	The Second World War	67
Ten.	The Cold War, Defending Gibraltar	76
Eleven.	A Canadian Refresher	82
Twelve.	Transporting the Spooks	86

Thirteen. Display Flying 1949	91
Fourteen. Display Flying 1989	97
Fifteen. Commandant and Air Officer Commanding	105
Sixteen. Station Commander	111
Seventeen. The Final Entries	117
ANNEX A A comparison of the aircraft	121
ANNEX B Record of Service	123
GLOSSARY OF TERMS	125
INDEX	127

40 photographic Plates will be found
betweem pages 60-61

FOREWORD

Despite its relatively recent evolution, flying seems to be in the blood of some families. The wonderment of flight has of course fascinated the human race for centuries but it is only in the last century that those dreams became a practical reality. Both my own and Tom Eeles' father served in the Royal Air Force in the early days before the Second World War. By a happy co-incidence my father, a flying instructor, taught Harry Eeles to fly at the RAF College at Cranwell in 1929. Over thirty years later, Tom Eeles and I joined the same Entry at Cranwell, and we have been firm friends ever since. Both fathers reached senior rank and each, in our own way, has flown in our father's slipstream, the apt title of this book.

This book tells of one family's RAF flying experience through flying operations during a greater part of the history of the Royal Air Force. Tom Eeles has cleverly, and for the first time, brought together two very different eras of flying for comparison; despite the many changes that have gone on, the love and adventure of flying remains unchanged. Tom Eeles has done this by studying the relevant pilot's flying logbooks. These are really an airman's diary of events, and much can be derived from their interpretation as becomes clear in this narrative. Despite the enormous advances in aviation in so short a period of time, there remains a bond between generations of flying men and women that is almost instinctively understood. This is a book about flying that anyone can enjoy and I commend it to you.

Air Marshal Sir Ian Macfadyen KCVO CB OBE
South Gloucestershire
January 2017

PREFACE

Military pilots are required to maintain a flying logbook recording all their flights in military aircraft. Because of the layout and space available, a pilot's flying logbook entries generally tend to be single line, very short statements of what a specific flight involved, for example 'Low level navigation', a typical entry that can be found often in my flying log book. However, I am convinced that behind many of these short entries there almost certainly lies a story worth telling. My father joined the RAF in 1929, in the age of biplanes that had not much changed since the First World War; in 1960 I followed him, the RAF now being firmly in the jet age. I finally hung up my flying helmet in 2010, eighty years after my father had started but with the RAF now firmly in the age of remotely piloted combat aircraft, digital networking and social media. After looking through his three and my four log books I have chosen seven entries from my father's which seemed to me the most interesting. I have tried to paint a picture of what each flight was like and also what was going on in the RAF and the wider world at the time. Sadly my father suffered badly from dementia in his latter years and like many of his generation was reticent about what he had done during his military service. He died in 1992, so inevitably I have had to use a degree of conjecture in describing the events surrounding each of his flights.

Having chosen seven entries from my father's logbooks, I have tried to find the nearest equivalent flights from my own logbooks. In a few cases it was surprising how close I was able to get to his experiences. One big difference was immediately apparent. Over a time span of twenty-nine years my father achieved 1374 hours flying; I was lucky enough to amass 8500 hours flying over fifty years. His service in the Second World War included only one rather short operational flying tour, his other appointments being mainly in command or staff positions involving little flying. I, on the other hand, was a Cold War participant, which gave me plenty of opportunity to get airborne. Both of us learnt our trade at the RAF College Cranwell, which had much changed between 1929 and 1960. We both led a nomadic life in our early years of RAF service. I was lucky enough to join the RAF when it still had a worldwide spread of permanent bases with resident squadrons although these were soon to disappear rapidly. My father's RAF was spread even further, as the sun did not set on the British Empire until the Second World War was over. Our combined experiences cover eighty years of the RAF's first century of existence.

My thanks are due to my great friend Air Marshal Sir Ian Macfadyen for agreeing to write the foreword to this book. Thanks also are due to Group Captain Nigel Walpole, a flight cadet at Cranwell during my father's time as Commandant, for his vivid description of what it was like to fly the Balliol. The books 'Flying Fever' by Air Vice-Marshal Stanley Vincent and 'A Pilot's Summer' by Group Captain Frank Tredrey provided invaluable quotes which I respectfully acknowledge. Finally I thank my wife Julia for putting up with my long absences at the laptop's keyboard.

I dedicate this book to my grandchildren, Walter, Amalfi, Harry and Olivia, to give them an idea of what flying was like for their great grandfather and grandfather in that first century of powered flight.

CHAPTER ONE

IN THE BEGINNING

LOGBOOK ENTRY, HARRY EELES

22 July 1929
Avro 504 J9012,
Flt Lt Macfadyen / Self,
Landing and Take Offs into wind, looping.
15 minutes, 2000 ft.

At first sight Harry Eeles, my father, might have been seen as an unlikely potential candidate for a career as a pilot and general duties officer in Trenchard's young Royal Air Force, which in 1929 had been in existence as an independent armed service for a mere 11 years. The Eeles family originally came from North Yorkshire where they were yeoman farmers, living in villages close to the River Tees some eight miles east of the town of Barnard Castle. Many of the family gravestones, dating back to the mid seventeenth century, can still be seen in the churchyard at Stanwick St John. In the middle of the nineteenth century the main branch of the family moved further north to Newcastle. Henry Eeles, Harry's father, went on a voyage from Cardiff to Odessa and back to Newcastle in 1878, writing a daily account of his experiences.

This diary is still in existence. As a consequence he became involved in the shipping industry and by 1909 was a ship owner and businessman of some substance in Newcastle. He married Florence Lloyd, niece of the Bishop of Newcastle, in 1906. Unfortunately he caught pneumonia as a result of being involved in a rescue attempt of the crew of one of his ships stranded on a

Tyneside beach during a storm in November 1909 and died aged only fifty-one. Harry Eeles was born on 12th May 1910, some seven months after his father had died. Harry was the youngest of three children and his widowed mother, Florence, soon moved from Newcastle to Kew to live near her sister, thus breaking the Eeles family's link with the north that had existed for very many years. In 1913 she met by chance a wealthy American widower, Francis Bond, who had two sons. Francis Bond and Florence Eeles married in 1914 and Francis Bond moved from Philadelphia to England, where he bought a small stately home, Wavendon House, just outside the present day city of Milton Keynes. He filled it with all his goods and chattels including a number of servants, horses, carriages and motor-cars. His youngest son James, aged 14, continued his education in England at Harrow and Trinity College, Cambridge, before returning to the USA where he became an expert ornithologist. He was always known as Jim Bond and kept in touch with his English stepsister and stepbrothers for the rest of his long life. Eventually he achieved some unexpected notoriety, as Ian Fleming admitted to stealing his name for use as the infamous hero James Bond in his racy spy novels.

Legend has it that Fleming was pacing around his study, trying to think of a suitable name for his hero, when he spotted a book in his library titled 'Birds of the Caribbean, by James Bond'; he decided on a whim that the name James Bond would do perfectly. After the publication of Fleming's Bond novels and the making of the first Bond films Jim and Mary Bond suddenly found life inexplicably difficult; every time Jim tried to book an airline ticket, a meal, a hire car or anything he was always replied with all sorts of innuendo that he did not understand, never having read any of the books or seen one of the films. Jim Bond and Fleming did once meet in Jamaica; Jim and his wife were passing Fleming's house 'Goldeneye' and decided on the spur of the moment to call in to see if this man who had made their life so difficult was at home. Hearing a degree of debate at the front door between the doorkeeper and the Bonds – the doorkeeper clearly not believing the name of the visitors – Fleming came to see what was happening and invited the unknown visitors in. Fleming and the real Bond evidently got on well together. Jim Bond was tall, slim and having been educated at Harrow and Cambridge was very English in manner and speech.

When the Bonds left Fleming presented Jim Bond with a copy of his latest novel, 'You Only Live Twice'. Inscribed on the fly leaf was 'To the real James Bond, from the thief of his identity, Ian Fleming, Feb. 5th 1964, a great day.' Mary Bond, Jim's wife, also wrote a small book titled 'How 007 Got His Name'.

A son, Peter, was born to Francis and Florence in 1918. Peter Bond also joined the RAF in 1938, doubtless as a result of his elder step brother Harry's influence. Peter Bond flew fighter aircraft throughout the Second World War, initially in India. By 1944 he had reached the rank of squadron leader and commanded a Spitfire squadron based in Kent, tasked with shooting down V1 flying bombs. By the end of the war he was a wing commander; he remained in the RAF after the end of hostilities and served as the wing leader of the Hornet squadrons based at RAF Horsham St Faith, now Norwich airport. He was killed in 1946 when, returning in a Hornet to Norfolk from a wedding in Swansea, he crashed in bad weather in the Brecon Beacons, having ignored advice to follow the better weather along the coast on his return flight.

Francis Bond never settled happily in England and died in 1923, leaving my grandmother his entire estate, but a widow yet again, although comfortably installed in Wavendon House where she remained until the late 1930s. My father followed his stepbrother and brother to Harrow School, and then surprised his family by deciding to join the Royal Air Force as a career officer and pilot through the newly established RAF College at Cranwell.

I do not know what it was that inspired him to do so. I still have in my possession an album full of postcards showing early aircraft and aviators from around 1910, originally collected by Jim Bond as a ten year old. Perhaps it was this, or the sight of aircraft flying over Harrow from the nearby airfields at Northolt and Hendon, I shall never know. Flying in 1929 was still considered by many to be a very risky occupation, the Royal Air Force itself was hardly a secure organization, being eyed with great jealousy by the other two armed services and suffering from a serious lack of Government funding. Thus I suspect that his twice widowed mother waved him off from Wavendon House to his new career in January 1929 with a high degree of trepidation.

Cranwell in 1929 was a sprawling hutted establishment on a bleak expanse of the Lincolnshire plateau, some twelve miles from the town of Grantham. It had been first developed as a Royal Naval Air Station during the First World War in 1915 as HMS Daedalus. There were two very large grass airfields north and south of the main camp, which was built either side of a minor public road. A railway branch line connected to the main line at the nearby town of Sleaford. Accommodation was mainly in primitive wooden huts, however, the Commandant lived in the relative luxury of The Lodge, originally a farmhouse requisitioned by the RN during the First World War and still retained today as the Commandant's residence. After the formation of the Royal Air Force by combining the Royal Naval Air Service and the Royal Flying Corps in 1918, Cranwell became an RAF Station. The Chief of the Air Staff, Marshal of the Royal Air Force Lord Trenchard, decided to establish three building blocks to support his infant air force, which would provide the core of the professional personnel for his young service and enable expansion to take place in the event of a crisis. He established a training school for apprentices at Halton to train his technicians, subsequently known as 'Trenchard's brats', a Cadet College for his career officer pilots at

Cranwell and a Staff College at Andover for their further education in high level staff work.

He chose the remote location of Cranwell for his Cadet College in the hope that it was too far from the fleshpots of London for the cadets to get there in their limited free time, unlike their opposite numbers at Sandhurst, so they would have to remain in Lincolnshire and concentrate on their professional studies. However, all Flight Cadets were issued with motor bikes which they were required to keep in a serviceable condition, it being felt essential that potential officers had to have enough mechanical knowledge to identify and even rectify faults in the unreliable aircraft of that period when flying in remote corners of the Empire. Thus the comforts of Wavendon House were not impossible to reach and a photograph (plate3) shows my father with his motorbike, proudly astride it outside the front door of Wavendon House, accompanied by his brother and younger stepbrother. The course at Cranwell was two years long and successful graduates were granted a permanent commission in the rank of Pilot Officer. All Flight Cadets were trained as pilots, there being at that time no separate specialization of navigator. Harry Eeles must have been considered a cadet of excellent military bearing, as he was chosen to be the model for the bronze 'maquette' that was used for the casting of the solid silver Ferris Trophy. The Ferris Trophy was the inter-squadron drill trophy and it shows a cadet, standing 'at ease', with a Lee Enfield rifle. I still have the 'maquette' in my possession.

Whilst life at Cranwell for the cadets must have been fairly similar to that at the public schools of the time, with the added rigour of military discipline, the great attraction for the cadets was the flying. Military flying training had been a very haphazard affair before and during the early years of the First World War, until a Major Smith-Barry, the commanding officer of 60 Squadron, complained so vehemently to higher authority about the poor quality of the pilots he was being sent, that in true British style higher authority sent him back to England to sort out the problem. Smith-Barry took over the training squadrons at Gosport, which became the School of Special Flying. The system of flying training which Smith-Barry developed there, which involved demonstration, instruction, practice and fault rectification, the use of instructional 'patter' and good communication between pupil and instructor using the 'Gosport Tube', has by and large survived intact to this day. The aircraft Smith-Barry's school used was the ubiquitous Avro 504 (plate1). The Avro 504 first flew in September 1913 and was well in advance of contemporary aircraft. It was widely used in a variety of operational roles by the RFC and the RNAS throughout the First World War. With the formation of the RAF in 1918 it continued in the training role, principally in the 'K' and 'N' versions, until the early 1930s. This was the aircraft that my father first flew at Cranwell in 1929 as a pupil. His instructor was a Flight Lieutenant Macfadyen, one of the flight commanders. Macfadyen went on to achieve high rank in the RAF; by coincidence his son Ian was on the same Cranwell Entry, 83, as myself and we have remained good friends ever since.

Those early training flights were all of fairly short duration, usually lasting no more than twenty to thirty minutes. Specific activities are recorded, such as in the example I have chosen, namely, 'Landings and take offs into wind, looping'. This seems a strange mixture of activity; normally aerobatics and circuit work do not mix well, especially on such a short flight of fifteen minutes at no higher than 2000 feet, but it is typical for that period. Perhaps the cold, draughty and noisy environment of the Avro 504's open cockpits militated against long instructional flights. As the course progressed other aircraft start to make an appearance in Harry Eeles's logbook. By late 1929 the venerable Bristol Fighter appears and in the spring of 1930 the Armstrong Whitworth Siskin, a front line fighter of the period, is recorded. By the end of the course a DH Moth and the Atlas, another Armstrong Whitworth product, feature. When he graduated in December 1930 my father had flown some forty-one hours dual and seventy-one hours solo on four different aircraft, the Avro 504, Bristol Fighter, Atlas and Siskin, a mixture of dual and solo flying totally different to that experienced by pilots in training in the twenty first century. His training as an officer and a pilot ready for front line service had taken just two years and in the sporting field he had learnt to fence to a high standard. He graduated twelfth out of a course of twenty-six. The senior term photograph (plate 2) of December 1930 shows him with three others in the rank of Flight Cadet Under Officer, the remainder being ranked Flight Cadet Sergeant or just Flight Cadet. Six of his Entry lost their lives in subsequent RAF service.

By way of comparison, the course at Cranwell today lasts only six months. Every individual, including females, seeking a commission in the RAF will undertake this course prior to commissioning. Specific training for pilots, engineers, administrators, in fact every specialization, takes place after graduation and can last a long time. The number of pilots amongst each entry is not great and their flying training starts with an elementary phase of some sixty hours. Following this they are separated into three different streams, helicopter, multi-engine or fast jet, depending on their individual skills and their own wishes. An increasing number will also be streamed into the role of remote piloting. Depending on which specialization they are selected for – fast jet, multi-engine or helicopter – flying training may well take up to three more years; quite a contrast to the less complex days of the 1930s.

CHAPTER TWO

CRANWELL IN THE 1960s

LOGBOOK ENTRY, TOM EELES

16 October 1961
Chipmunk T10
Self
First solo
20 minutes

There was a two-year gap from 1958, when my father retired from the RAF (see Chapter 15), until September 1960 when I arrived at the RAF College Cranwell. Those two years were turbulent and filled with incident. After a childhood spent on two RAF stations I was determined to become a pilot in the RAF. Aged fifteen, whilst at Sherborne School, I applied for selection to join the RAF as a pilot and after visiting the Selection Boards at RAF Hornchurch and Daedalus House at Cranwell I was awarded an RAF Scholarship. This helped with the school fees and guaranteed a place at the RAF College provided a suitable number of O and A level GCE exam passes were achieved. I was an enthusiastic member of the school's Combined Cadet Force (CCF) RAF Section.

Being fairly close to RAF Boscombe Down meant that the RAF CCF members visited this establishment quite often and flew in a variety of aircraft such as the Chipmunk, Meteor and Beverley transport. I was even lucky enough to get a flight in a two seat Hunter, an experience that introduced me not only to a short spell of supersonic flight but also 'g' induced loss of consciousness during recovery from the supersonic dive. After passing enough O levels my future career depended on achieving at least a pass in two A levels, the necessary minimum standard required for entry into Cranwell; at some risk I only attempted to study for two subjects, as there was too much else to enjoy outside the classroom. In 1959 the RAF section spent its summer camp at RAF Laarbruch in Germany where more flying in the station flight Chipmunk and Meteor took place. I also flew as a passenger in a Canberra B(I)8 of 16 Squadron on a night sortie. Little did I realize that I would be a member of this squadron only some four years later, and doubtless fly this aircraft as its pilot. All this 'air experience' was to stand me in good stead in the future.

Back at home my mother was suffering from cancer, but the seriousness of her illness was never really brought home to my brother, sister and I. My father was attempting to start a new career after being forced to retire from the RAF but the pressures of looking after my ailing mother and the needs of three teenage children were too much for any success in this endeavour. Then in January 1960 I was called out of a lesson to be told that my mother had died. The next few days and weeks were something of a blur but eventually it was time to sit the dreaded A levels. I left Sherborne at the end of the summer term to await the results of my A levels, which were dispatched by telegram to where we were staying in Yorkshire on a family holiday. Relief – pass in both subjects, so now it was time to get ready for entry into the RAF College Cranwell.

The RAF College in the 1960s was competing with the universities for top quality entrants. Flight Cadets spent three years at the College, the course was now three years long and there were three terms in each year, just like a university. The academic syllabus was split three ways. The 'A' stream was a purely 'in house' RAF general studies syllabus designed for those students who had not shown any particular academic flair on their O and A level courses. The 'B' stream was for those who were of a scientific bent and at the end of the course they finished by taking an exam set by the Royal Aeronautical Society, a pass conferring membership as an Associate Fellow. The 'C' stream was for those who specialized in the humanities – history, languages and military studies – the course syllabus and final exams were set by the University of London, with the award of Bachelor of Arts for those who passed. This academic hotchpotch was an attempt to make the RAF College equivalent to a university with a degree qualification after a three-year course, in order to attract those who were put off by the lack of a professional qualification offered by Cranwell other than a flying brevet. I was placed in the C stream to study history, military history and English language; it was difficult to be enthusiastic about learning how to interpret Anglo Saxon grammar whilst one's fellow Flight Cadets were being taught something far more appropriate to their military flying careers. On top of this academic rigueur was all the military training – drill, customs and traditions of the Service, leadership, fitness, combat survival, air force law, nuclear and biological warfare and of course flying training.

Flying training was the great attraction for us all, flying was what had encouraged us in the first place into joining the RAF, just as it had done for our predecessors in the 1920s. Unfortunately there was no flying training at all during the first year of the course. The first term at Cranwell was something of a culture shock, even for those like myself from a service background who had some rough idea of what it might be like. Despite arriving with short haircuts our hair was immediately shortened even further. We were left in no doubt about our lowly status as the junior entry. Our accommodation was in the South Brick Lines, primitive huts dating from the First World War that had hardly changed since then. The linoleum floors had to be kept shining so we slid around on them on felt pads. The only heating was a coke-fuelled stove in the middle of the sleeping area that made a terrible mess when lit, but it was the only form of heating and Lincolnshire gets very cold in the winter. Everything had to be kept immaculate in the hut. Clothes and personal kit had to be laid out precisely without variation from the official diagram. Any fault found ended with the victim being placed on 'Restrictions', an added burden as one had to appear three times a day for inspection and drill, in addition to the busy routine of the normal day's training activity. The uniform was shapeless hairy battle dress with white webbing, all of which had to be perfectly sparkling all the time. It was a high-pressure environment designed to test us to the limit and not all those who arrived on day one made it through to the end of the first term. After the first term conditions improved somewhat in that we moved from the huts to a barrack block with single rooms and central heating, but the inspection routine was much the same. At least it was easier to keep a single room up to the required standard of cleanliness and layout.

A new entry of cadets moved into the South Brick Lines and each hut had a mentor provided from the entry above to show the new boys the ropes. I got lumbered as a mentor so had two terms in the huts rather than the normal one. Cars were allowed from the second term onwards. This was before the days of the annual MoT test so a wide variety of unreliable cars dating mainly from the 1930s and 40s could be found in the cadet's garage, a large hangar also dating from the First World War. Despite the mobility offered by car ownership we lived a fairly cloistered life at Cranwell, only being allowed out off duty on Saturday evenings and Sundays after Church Parade. Occasional weekend passes had to be applied for by formal official letter starting ' Sir, I have the honour to request…' We were allowed three each term and most were spent in London. The 'Swinging Sixties' were just starting and the draw exerted by London was hard to resist, provided your car did not break down on the way there. Lord Trenchard would surely not have approved of these expeditions to 'the smoke.'

Another bonus in the second and third terms was the introduction of air experience flying once a week in the Chipmunk. The Chipmunk (plate 4) was, and still is, a delightfully traditional elementary trainer. Powered by a Gypsy Major engine, with a fixed tail wheel undercarriage and tandem seating, it was the product initially of de Havilland's Canadian subsidiary. Built in large numbers by de Havilland in the UK, it served for very many years in the RAF as an elementary trainer, equipping many Flying Training Schools, University Air Squadrons and Air Experience Flights. Two are still in use today on the Battle of Britain Memorial Flight and there are many flying on the civil register. It is an easy aircraft to fly but it is difficult to fly well. The cockpit layout was rather haphazard, with the brake lever on the left hand side being awkward to use and the flap selector on the right needing a change of hands on the control column to select flap, inevitably at a critical stage of the final approach. A cartridge starter using cartridges similar to those found with a twelve-bore shotgun started the engine. After strapping in and checking around the cockpit, you would extend your arms outside so they could be seen not to be fiddling with anything by your ground crew. You would then shout 'Fuel on, brakes on, throttle closed, switches safe.'

The ground crew would pump some fuel into the carburetor by hand, install the starter cartridge and secure the cowlings, and respond with 'Cowlings secure, starter fitted, clear to start', or words to that effect. You would then withdraw your arms into the cockpit, advance the throttle a small amount, put the magneto switches to live, ensure that the brakes were firmly on, hold the control column fully rearward with your left hand and with your right hand pull the starter operating chain which was somewhat similar to that used on an overhead lavatory cistern. With a bit of luck, after a loud explosion the engine would start. To set the brakes for taxiing you had to release the hand brake, apply rudder then apply two or three notches of hand brake, this gave braking to each wheel with an input of rudder movement. Taxiing required regular weaving to see what there was in front of you. One could almost imagine oneself to be in a World War Two fighter. Once airborne the Chipmunk was great fun for aerobatics and cruised at a stately 90 knots. Landing in a cross- wind could be challenging, needing good co-ordination of control column, rudder and throttle inputs. In fact its overall performance and handling qualities were not too dissimilar from the Avro 504s based at Cranwell in 1929.

The Chipmunk Flight at Cranwell flew from the grass North Airfield, apparently the largest open space in Lincolnshire. The South Airfield, with its hard runways, was reserved for the more important proper flying training activities of Cranwell's Jet Provost fleet. Once a week we would report to the Chipmunk Flight for our one flight. Most of the Chipmunk pilots were on ground tours at the College and only a few were qualified as Chipmunk Qualified Flying Instructors (QFIs). Only Chipmunk QFIs could fly in the rear seat and give proper instruction, so most of the time we sat in the back and had to put up with aerobatics being flown by the man in the front. As a consequence all the Chipmunks exuded a distinct aroma of vomit, thus the more sensitive of our company did not really look forward to this weekly event. If you were lucky enough to fly with a QFI you sat in the front and were actually taught to fly rather than just watch.

With no specific runways being marked out on the enormous grass airfield we never had to land cross wind. I was lucky in that I got a few flights with a QFI and my logbook records that on 16th October 1961, after eight hours thirty minutes dual over a period of nearly ten months, Flt Lt Ayers sent me off solo. I really do not recall anything of the sortie, which consisted of a simple take off, circuit and landing but obviously I must have completed it without incident. I only flew the Chipmunk two more times at Cranwell, both flights in the back seat. Our proper flying training started in January 1962 on the Jet Provost. I did not fly the Chipmunk again for twenty-seven years, until 1988, but I subsequently accumulated quite a number of hours in it at CFS, Linton on Ouse and Cambridge, both as a QFI and an Air Experience Flight pilot. I have very happy memories of the Chipmunk, it is a truly classic aircraft.

The flying done in the Chipmunk counted for nothing once Jet Provost flying started. The RAF introduced 'all through' jet flying training with the Jet Provost, the first air force in the world to do so. By 1962 this system was in full operation at Cranwell, using two versions of the Jet Provost, the Mk 3 and Mk 4. The Mk 3 had a less powerful engine than the Mk 4 but otherwise the two aircraft were virtually identical. We started on the Mk 3, which had a fairly pedestrian performance and was once described as 'the constant thrust, variable noise machine'. Nevertheless it represented quite an advance on the Chipmunk, with retractable landing gear, ejection seats, an oxygen system and the ability to get up to about 25,000 ft, albeit somewhat slowly. The photograph (plate 5) shows the extensive flight line at Cranwell in those days. Note that the flight cadets, in their light blue flying suits, are all wearing collars and ties. The Mk 4, with its more powerful engine, was a much more lively aircraft well capable of getting beyond 30,000 ft. It was a popular aircraft for aerobatics and high-level formation sorties were a regular feature until the medics became so concerned about the effects of decompression sickness in an unpressurised aircraft that another version of the Jet Provost appeared. This was the Mk 5, with a redesigned forward fuselage and a pressurised cockpit. It retained the Mk4's engine but with pressurisation air being tapped off it, it fell a bit short of the Mk 4's performance.

Despite our flying training finally starting in January 1962 parades, drill, service training and of course for me the continuing study for my BA took place alongside the flying. In the autumn of 1962 the world outside was slowly sliding into what might have been a potential third world war, fought with nuclear weapons, with the start of the Cuban missile crisis. We were aware of what was going on through the TV news and the papers, but our more immediate concerns were to avoid being re-coursed through some failure in flying or academic work, or worse still 'the chop' for complete failure. The gravity of the international situation was only brought home to us when we observed from the cockpits of our JPs that the ballistic missile sites scattered about Lincolnshire had all their Thor missiles, equipped with nuclear warheads, erected with liquid oxygen venting from them. This indicated that they were at a very short notice to be launched. Normally just one might occasionally be seen erected at a single site, but for a short time every one was up and ready. Nevertheless we carried on trying to impress our flying instructors with our flying skills and in my case struggling with Anglo Saxon scripts.

Eventually the crisis passed and we finally graduated from Cranwell some nine months later in July 1963, marching up the steps of the College to Auld Lang's Syne and swapping our Flight Cadet's uniform for Pilot Officer's, resplendent with pilot's wings that had been presented to us the night before by Air Marshal Sir 'Gus' Walker, the C in C of Flying Training Command, and the thin blue stripe of a Pilot Officer. Just before finishing the course I took my final exams for BA in London. However, the College authorities had told us candidates that it didn't really matter how well or badly we performed, we would graduate regardless. Thus two weeks in London were most enjoyably spent without much academic revision, including sailing a yacht from Dover to the Hamble over a weekend. I did pass, but not very well, getting a third class degree. Unlike my father, our next destination was not a front line squadron but yet another flying training course, to be followed by an operational conversion course on a front line aircraft before joining a squadron. The days of moving directly to a front line squadron from Cranwell had long gone.

CHAPTER THREE

THE BEST FLYING CLUB IN THE WORLD

LOGBOOK ENTRY, HARRY EELES

18 July 1932
Bulldog K2190
Self
Sector G, night patrol, Command exercises
Forced landing due to weather at Reading 'drome.
Burst tyre and damaged starboard wing.
1 hour 10 minutes, 2000ft

Let me turn again to Harry Eeles, who was posted to No 41 Fighter Squadron on graduation from Cranwell in January 1931, still aged only twenty. The Squadron was based at RAF Northolt on the outskirts of London and equipped with the Armstrong Whitworth Siskin, a fighter aircraft with which he would have been fully familiar with, having flown it often during his flying training at Cranwell. In the 1930s the RAF's fighter squadrons were considered by many to be the best flying clubs in the world, equipped as they were with glamorous silver biplanes covered with bright squadron colours. They were not much different to the fighting scouts of the RFC. Doubtless another bonus was being based at Northolt, a mere stone's throw from the delights of London's West End and within easy reach of his home at Wavendon. However, it appears that all was not sweetness and light on 41 Fighter Squadron.

Not long after Harry Eeles's arrival Squadron Leader S F Vincent took over command of the squadron in September 1931. Vincent had been a young fighter pilot in the RFC and by the end of the First World War had distinguished himself both as a fighter pilot and a flying instructor, serving in France with 60 Squadron and with Major Smith-Barry at the School of Special Flying, Gosport. Vincent wrote his excellent autobiography 'Flying Fever', published by Jarrolds, in 1972. To quote directly from it: '*I was posted to take over No 41 Squadron at Northolt, also with Siskins but fairly soon converted to Bristol Bulldogs. I found the Squadron very un-fighter minded; aerobatics and formation flying were sadly neglected. I had to work hard with competitions for the former and regular days every week for the latter, until they slowly became a good squadron.*' Thus Vincent's arrival must have been something of a shock to 41 Squadron. My father found himself appointed Squadron Adjutant by Vincent, probably as a consequence of his Cranwell training but a clear indication of his administrative ability. He collected a brand new Bulldog, K2182, from the Bristol Aeroplane Company's factory at Filton (plate 7) on 30th October 1931 and the Siskin soon disappears from his logbook.

The Bristol Bulldog (plate 6) first flew in 1927. It was built as a fast light fighter able to catch the new generation of fast bombers. Over four hundred were built and many were exported to eight other countries. It was undoubtedly one of the finest aerobatic biplanes ever made. It was powered by a 440hp Bristol Jupiter radial engine and represented a big advance on the elderly Siskin. An example that has survived can be seen in the RAF Museum at Hendon. However, whilst it must have been a wonderful aircraft to fly by day, it was probably not much fun to fly at night.

So let me turn to this logbook entry. Cockpit instruments had not advanced much over the previous decade. There was no blind flying panel as such, so no artificial horizon or attitude indicator. The altimeter would have been a single needle instrument prone to many errors, there was no indication of vertical velocity and the compass would also have been plagued by errors. These few instruments were scattered somewhat randomly around the instrument panel and were probably not well lit. Thus night flying would have been a challenging experience. Airfield lighting was very primitive, consisting of 'goose-neck' flares (large metal cans with a spout, filled with paraffin) to indicate the best take off and landing direction on the grass airfield, but little else. It is quite likely that even this primitive lighting might not have been available at Reading, a civilian airfield. 'Command Exercises' were beginning to feature more often in the early 1930s as the RAF struggled to devise a system to enable fighters to intercept incoming bombing raids. This was the era of the much-quoted statement by Prime Minister Stanley Baldwin that 'the bomber will always get through' and memories of the raids on London by the Germans during the First World War were still fresh in many people's minds.

Evidence of these raids can still be seen in the damage caused to the lion statues at Cleopatra's Needle on the Thames Embankment. Nevertheless, slow progress was being made. Attempts to locate aircraft approaching from the continent were made using enormous concrete sound mirrors, some of which still survive on the south coast to this day; these were not very successful. To quote S F Vincent again, *'With No 41 came Radio Telephony (R/T) – that is, speech replaced the Morse signals of Wireless Telegraphy (W/T) used hitherto. Our sets, on medium wave bands, had to be adjusted by pilots to a high degree of sensitivity, so that conversations between air and ground and air to air was doubtful and there was considerable interference from adjacent channels and other 'noises off'.'* Vincent also describes how trials at this period started for the control of fighters from the ground. *'The squadron had a small Operations Room, in which a controller gave instructions to the Fighter Leader by Radio Telephony, through the medium of an airman operator. On one occasion the order 'Patrol Halton 15,000 feet' was passed on by a Cockney airman operator as 'Patrol 'Alton 15,000 feet.' The Fighter Leader duly led his formation down to Hampshire instead of Buckinghamshire and two early lessons were learned, one, the controller must give the orders himself, and two, that place names on the map are useless.'* Interestingly, during refurbishment of a small brick building at RAF Northolt a few years ago a section of the wooden wall map of southern England used in this early Operations Room was found in a skip and recovered for display. Trying to cope with this new technology whilst flying a skittish aerobatic biplane at night, in bad weather, then having to divert to a civilian airfield must have been a challenging experience. A burst tyre and a damaged wing are hardly surprising under these circumstances. Clearly the damage was speedily repaired, as he was airborne again the following morning in K2190 on a transit flight of twenty minutes from Reading to Northolt.

A few more years were to pass before a working system of early warning and fighter control was established, thanks to the invention of Radio Direction Finding, otherwise known as Radar, the founding of the Observer Corps and the initiation of the Dowding System for controlling fighters being in place just in time for the outbreak of the Second World War. A month after the incident at Reading airfield my father moved on to an entirely different scene, with an assessment from his squadron commander of 'Well Above the Average on Siskins and Bulldogs'. S F Vincent had a very long career in the RAF, serving with distinction at home and overseas in the Second World War, finally retiring as an Air Vice-Marshal. After the Second World War he was Air Officer Commanding No 11 Group, Fighter Command, when Harry Eeles was commanding one of his major fighter bases, as described in Chapter Thirteen.

CHAPTER FOUR

NEARLY THE BEST FLYING CLUB IN THE FAR EAST

LOGBOOK ENTRY, TOM EELES

13 May 1965
Canberra B(I)8 XK 952
Self/ Flt Lt Avery
Day and night shallow dive bombing under flares
China Rock Range
1 hour 5 minutes day, 1 hour 5 minutes night

After finishing my flying training in March 1964 I was posted to fly the Canberra, a light bomber employed in the tactical role at overseas RAF bases in Germany. Tension between the West and the Soviet Union was running high, with the drama of the Cuban Missile crisis very fresh in everyone's memory. At this time the RAF still had a sizeable Tactical Air Force based in West Germany as part of the United Kingdom's military contribution to the NATO Alliance. There were a couple of air defence squadrons equipped with Gloster Javelin all-weather fighters, which were soon replaced by Lightnings, and two fighter reconnaissance squadrons equipped with Hunters. Two further squadrons were equipped with the photo-reconnaissance version of the Canberra, and four squadrons of Canberra light bombers, which provided the tactical punch.

The Canberra could carry a single nuclear bomb, which was delivered from a low level high speed run in to the target, throwing the bomb forward from a looping manoeuvre, which theoretically would allow the aircraft to escape the worst effects of the subsequent nuclear blast. This was known as the Low Altitude Bombing System, or LABS. The ability to carry out what was in effect an aerobatic manoeuvre, a roll off the top of a loop, from as low as two hundred and fifty feet, legally, had a certain attraction to us young pilots. I was posted to No 16 Squadron, which was based at RAF Laarbruch, situated close to the Dutch border between the Rhine and Maas rivers. The squadron was equipped with the B(I)8 version of the Canberra, (the I stood for Interdictor), which was somewhat different to all the previous marks. The pilot sat on an ejection seat under a fighter type bubble canopy, which afforded excellent all round visibility but perversely could not be opened, so the internal temperature could reach very high levels even in winter. There was only one navigator, who had no ejection seat, and who lived in the dark recesses of the forward fuselage. His only means of escape in an emergency was to bale out of the entrance door and open his parachute manually, not a pleasant prospect when most of our flying was carried out at very low levels. His flying suit had a parachute harness integrated within it along with an emergency oxygen bottle, which made the whole ensemble bulky, uncomfortable and hot. For visual navigation he lay on a couch looking out of a Perspex nose cone, a position extremely vulnerable to the bird strikes which occurred regularly. He also occupied this position during LABS manoeuvres and was not strapped in. How the long-suffering navigators endured this uncomfortable and risky existence I will never know.

The tactical nuclear strike role in support of NATO was the principal task of RAF Germany's four Canberra squadrons. This involved extensive training in LABS bombing and included the burdensome task of each squadron maintaining two aircraft on Quick Reaction Alert at all times. There was an additional complication in that the nuclear weapon was provided by the USA under a 'dual key' arrangement. Thus to be released on a war mission the approval of both the US and UK authorities would have been needed, a considerable challenge under the stress of a potential third World War.

However, the squadrons also had a secondary role not associated with NATO, in support of purely national UK tasks. In this role the Canberra B(I)8 became a large ground attack aircraft, carrying a gun pack in the rear half of the bomb bay fitted with four 20mm cannon. Sixteen flares could be carried in the front half of the bomb bay to illuminate targets at night, together with two conventional 1000 lb high explosive bombs carried on the two wing pylons. There was no bombsight fitted to this mark of Canberra so the pilot had a simple ring and bead type of gun sight to deliver his bombs or bullets in dive attack profiles. Day and night dive bombing and air to ground gunnery were practiced only twice a year at three week long Armament Practice Camps; generally you had to have been on the squadron for at least a year before you were allowed to take part in this demanding and exciting sort of flying.

In the early 1960s there was trouble brewing out in the Far East. The communist insurgency of the 1950s in Malaya had been defeated but a new threat had arisen. The Malaysian Federation, consisting of Malaya, Singapore and parts of Borneo including Labuan and Brunei found itself under serious threat of military attack from the administration led by the dictatorial President Sukarno that governed Indonesia. This became known as Indonesian Confrontation. The UK maintained very close relationships with the Malaysian Federation, with significant air, sea and land military forces committed to the area. The Royal Malaysian Air Force (RMAF) had been formed, very much on RAF lines, but at that time had only a very limited light transport capability. The RAF had a major presence in the Far East, with a large Headquarters and three airfields on Singapore Island at Tengah, Changi and Seletar with air defence, ground attack, support helicopter and transport squadrons all based permanently on the island. There was a staging post in the Indian Ocean on the island of Gan in the Maldives, a presence also in Hong Kong and a number of reserve airfields in mainland Malaya and in Borneo and

Sarawak. By the middle of 1964 the Indonesian Confrontation was in full swing, with many skirmishes taking place in Borneo, infiltration by Indonesian Special Forces into the Malay Peninsula and the ever-present possibility of a full-scale minor war breaking out.

In November 1964 16 Squadron was selected to detach nine aircraft to Malaya to reinforce the Far East Air Force. The squadron would be stood down from its QRA commitment, leaving only a few crews remaining back at Laarbruch to continue with normal training. Despite never having done any conventional weapons training, I saw this unexpected deployment as a possibly unique once in a lifetime opportunity to experience some real operational action in an exotic and exciting part of the world. This was just the sort of activity that I had joined the RAF to get involved in. I begged the squadron commander to let me go, in any capacity, despite my inexperience in conventional weapon delivery and very junior status; much to my great surprise and delight he agreed. After a few attempts at some conventional weapons delivery profiles at the Nordhorn weapons range in Germany, I flew out to join the squadron courtesy of RAF Transport Command in a Britannia transport aircraft. It was a journey that took quite a long time, with a number of stops en route in Malta, Cyprus and Bahrain, where I was bumped off the aircraft to make way for a more senior individual. There was no likelihood of suffering from jet lag on this journey. Eventually I found a seat in a Comet transport aircraft that completed the flight via the island airfield at Gan in the Maldives to Changi, the RAF's transport hub in Singapore, where I was met by some of the squadron aircrew and taken immediately into the fleshpots of Singapore's notorious Bugis Street. It is best to draw a discreet veil over the subsequent proceedings. The next day we flew on up country in a Valetta transport aircraft to the squadron's operating base, the bare base reserve airfield at Kuantan, some 150 miles north of Singapore on the east coast of Malaya.

Because of the overcrowding at RAF Tengah, the main offensive support airfield on Singapore Island, 16 Squadron was based at the emergency airfield at Kuantan (plate 8). Compared to the luxury of the squadron's permanent home in Germany, Kuantan was a very primitive establishment. It had originally been built in the 1930s as a grass airfield, taken over and expanded by the Japanese in World War 2 and given a single runway six thousand feet long. The Japanese infrastructure had by now disappeared into the jungle; the only permanent buildings were a small wooden air traffic control tower used by the civilian controllers when the Malaysian Airlines Dakota flew in and out, and an associated fire engine shed. The large RAF detachment all lived and worked under canvas. The tents were of considerable vintage, dating from the end of the Second World War. Accommodation was in two-man tents and there was a large marquee (plate 9) that served as the Officers' Mess and bar. In many ways it certainly resembled a pre-war flying club. Meals were cooked in a communal facility with a corrugated tin roof but open sides, there was a rudimentary electricity supply that provided a few lights but not much else.

Slit trenches abounded everywhere and the airfield's defences consisted of a few rather old 20mm anti aircraft guns that had once been used to defend Singapore's naval dockyard. Communal washing facilities and chemical toilets of the Racasan variety were provided behind canvas screens. The toilet seats were notoriously flimsy and soon split, so it was important to watch out for the morning delivery of new toilets and grab one early to avoid being nipped sharply on the posterior. There was no television or telephone apart from two phone lines, solely for operational use, routed to the exchange in the town of Kuantan, some five miles away. The internet, personal computers, ipads and mobile phones had not been invented. A rudimentary outdoor cinema was used to show films provided from Singapore, to keep all personnel amused during the evenings. The tropical jungle came right up to the edge of the campsite, with its large population of snakes, insects and other more dangerous beasts, some of which regularly infiltrated the camp. Dress codes were very relaxed, especially when compared to our more formal existence back at Laarbruch. Most of the time we just wore casual shirts, shorts and flip-flops, only changing reluctantly into more formal Khaki Drill (KD) tropical uniform if a VIP from Singapore was about to visit.

Because of the unusual nature of the airfield at Kuantan when compared to normal RAF bases, we had many curious visitors. Sometimes our visitors would stay overnight. Darkness arrived quickly in the tropics so the visitor would be offered a Tiger beer or two when the bar in the marquee opened at 1800hrs. By the time he had consumed these it would be very dark, so he would be sent out into the night to find his tent and, naturally in an Officers' Mess however rudimentary, change for dinner. We all hoped he would stumble over the sand bagged edge of a slit trench and fall into the trench, which was now full of water from the regular afternoon storm. On one unforgettable day, when the Command Fire Officer visited to inspect our fire fighting facilities, the camp field kitchen obligingly caught fire and burnt out in front of him.

The conduct of flying operations was delightfully relaxed, compared to what it was like in Germany. There was no formal Air Traffic Control, as none was really needed, 16 Squadron being the sole flying unit at the airfield. Occasional visitors from Singapore arrived either in Bristol Freighters flown by the RNZAF or RAF Valettas. There were also visits from the RNZAF squadron equipped with the export version of the Canberra B(I)8, the B(I)12, which, frustratingly, was better equipped than our aircraft. All the aircraft were parked in the open on frying pan style hard standings, so were vulnerable to the vagaries of the weather, most often torrential rain and thunderstorms. There was also a large hangar rather reminiscent of a circus 'big top' tent where aircraft servicing protected from the weather could take place. The squadron's role was to provide long range day and night interdiction, using the 20mm cannon and 1000lb conventional bombs. Our night capability was somewhat rudimentary. The most likely targets, should Confrontation escalate into a genuine war, would have been Indonesian airfields and military facilities on the island of Sumatra. Our training sorties consisted of tactical formation flying and navigation, weapons training by day and night on the local weapons ranges at China Rock, Asahan and Song Song, and practice airfield attacks back at Kuantan. Compared to the rather more formal and serious style of flying in Germany, and for myself so recently out of the closely supervised world of flying training it was a refreshing and exciting business.

Let me turn now to my chosen logbook entry. Whilst day flying at Kuantan was pretty straightforward, night flying was somewhat more challenging and more akin to what my father had experienced all those years before at Northolt. The runway was equipped with a series of electric lights along its edges but these were of very low intensity, unreliable and were difficult to make out from a distance. Therefore a number of gooseneck flares were used to enhance the visibility of the flare path, but for some reason there were not enough to line each side of the runway. It was therefore essential to remember which side they were on before landing to avoid touching down on the grass. There was no facility for radar approaches and the nights in the tropics were very dark, as there was not much cultural lighting nearby. Shortly after my arrival at Kuantan the first night sortie to a weapons range to practice dive bombing under flares took place, the crew selected being the most experienced in this type of work. They were to use China Rock range, the target was an isolated rock in the sea close to the coast north east of Singapore, but because of the threat of night time incursions by Indonesian commandos the range safety party was always withdrawn during the hours of darkness. The crew therefore had to carry out what was known as 'clear range procedure', making sure by themselves that it was safe to drop any ordinance. They were eagerly questioned on their return to Kuantan as to how they had got on. They admitted to dropping all 16 flares, but declared that they had decided not to drop any practice bombs as they had great difficulty in identifying the target rock.

The next morning the two phone lines into the airfield rapidly became overloaded with calls from HQ FEAF demanding explanations. Apparently most of the flares' parachutes had drifted onto the mainland and, when dawn broke, were found by local villagers who assumed that a supply drop to infiltrating Indonesians had taken place. A major security alert ensued, until the culprits were identified at Kuantan enjoying a late breakfast. This explains why my logbook entry includes quite a long period of day flying in addition to the night element. Given the need to identify positively the unlit China Rock, this really could only be done in daylight, as the Canberra B(I)8's navigation equipment was not suited to precise fixing in this part of the world. The Decca fixing system, which was very accurate, needed a ground-based chain of beacons and there was no such facility in Malaya. The only other navigation aid was a Doppler system, called Blue Silk, but many were not reliable by now as there were very few spares for it available at Kuantan, the other Canberras permanently based in the Far East having a different system. Thus a map and eyeball became our most accurate navigation aids, a situation not much different from my father's night flying experience in the early 1930s. My recollection is that we found the range and carried out a few dry passes in the remaining daylight, then dropped our flares, four at a time, and had a go at dive bombing under their rather feeble illumination. The results of our attempts remain a mystery as their was no range party to provide a score. Finally we made our way back to Kuantan, found the airfield and landed on the right side of the flares, to retire ultimately to the Officers' Mess tent for a welcome glass of Tiger. Making one's way back to the tent to sleep, it was important not to trip over a sand bag lined slit trench and fall in, as the trench would still be full of rain water from the regular late afternoon downpour.

Eventually it was time to return to Laarbruch and the rigours of QRA, our place at Kuantan being taken by a Canberra squadron from Cyprus. As the aircraft had been without wing-tip tanks fitted to allow them to carry out weapon delivery without a low 'g' limitation, the tanks had to be refitted and checked out on long, boring flights at high level, to ensure the fuel fed through satisfactorily before we set off across the Indian Ocean. As I was the most junior member of the squadron many of these flights fell to me. Our route home was Kuantan – Butterworth – Gan – Masirah – Bahrain – Cyprus – Malta – Laarbruch, with a night stop at each location, the ground crew following us in a Britannia. Of these locations only Cyprus now retains an RAF presence. Again, this was quite an experience for me, with long ocean crossings in an aircraft with very limited navigation aids and a leg skirting the southern fringes of the Soviet Union over Turkey, where attempts to seduce aircraft over the border were commonplace. We flew in pairs, each separated by about five minutes, I was number two to the squadron commander who naturally was the first off every morning. There was actually no need to visit Masirah but the leading pair elected to do so. I asked my navigator why we were diverting to this solitary outpost off the coast of the Sultanate of Oman. He replied that it was the best place in the Middle East to buy desert boots and he guessed that the squadron commander needed a new pair.

We had to carry out a few low passes to scatter the goats and camels off the runway, the squadron commander bought his desert boots, we had a meal in the Officers' Mess and were shown the door marked 'BBC TV Room' which opened out on to the desert, then carried on to Bahrain. Our final leg from Malta to Laarbruch was carried out as a diamond nine formation on the squadron commander's insistence, with a fly-by at Laarbruch to announce our return. I had gained a great deal of experience by the time we had all landed, in less than a year after finishing my flying training. Life back at Laarbruch was inevitably rather staid after all this, so when the opportunity came along to volunteer for loan service with the Fleet Air Arm I applied, much to the astonishment of the older and wiser squadron members who could not understand why I wanted to swap nine thousand feet of concrete runway that never moved for seven hundred feet of mobile elderly aircraft carrier. The four months I spent in Malaya were an unforgettable experience that I remember with great pleasure.

CHAPTER FIVE

HARD WORK IN THE DESERT

LOGBOOK ENTRY, HARRY EELES

17 June 1933
Fairey IIIF J9155
Self/Air Officer Commanding
Khartoum to Ed Damer, 1hour, 35 minutes, 4000ft
Ed Damer to Atbara, 5 minutes, 1000ft
Atbara to Ed Damer, 10minutes, 1000ft
Ed Damer to Wadi Halfa, 3hours, 55minutes, 7000ft

As a young officer on a permanent commission Harry Eeles was quite likely to be selected for some other form of service appointment quite different from that of a fighter pilot on a home-based squadron. After nearly two years on 41 Squadron, he was chosen to be the Aide de Camp (ADC) to Air Vice-Marshal Cyril Newall, the Air Officer Commanding (AOC) the RAF in the Middle East, whose Headquarters were at Heliopolis in Egypt. This was a prestigious and high profile appointment but with many potential pitfalls. An ADC was responsible for managing his master's work and social diary, writing his speeches, dealing with all sorts of varied requests including those concerned with domestic arrangements and the needs of the AOC's wife, and last but not least, in the 1930s being the AOC's personal pilot.

The reader may wonder now why on earth the British had such a large military presence in Egypt in the early years of the twentieth century, which although not actually a British colony might well have been mistaken for one at that time. Admiral Lord

Nelson had destroyed the French fleet at Aboukir Bay during the Napoleonic Wars but the British did not get closely involved with Egypt at that time. This all changed with the construction of the Suez Canal. Owned jointly by the British and French, it was the vital lifeline that enabled Great Britain to communicate easily with its Empire in India (the Jewel in the Crown), the Far East, Australia and New Zealand, without ships having to undertake the long, expensive and hazardous voyage around the Cape of Good Hope in South Africa. Egypt was nominally an independent kingdom but by the 1930s could easily have been mistaken for a British colony. The British military presence in Egypt lasted until the 1950s when the RAF finally left what was known as the Canal Zone. In 1956 President Nasser, who had ousted the king of Egypt in a coup, nationalized the Suez Canal, thereby precipitating an ill conceived Anglo/French military campaign to recover it, in connivance with the Israelis. Although militarily successful it proved to be a political and diplomatic disaster and marked, amongst other things, the end of active British military involvement in Egypt.

Shortly after the Armistice in November 1918, the threat to the continuing existence and independence of the RAF by the Treasury, the Royal Navy and the Army was very real, but the opportunity to provide 'Air Control' in the turbulent tribal regions of Iraq, Mesopotamia, Palestine, Trans Jordan and Egypt was grasped eagerly by Trenchard, the Chief of the Air Staff. He was able to show how a fairly small number of aircraft and personnel could police the region's dissident tribesmen at a far lesser cost than the traditional use of large numbers of troops; this proved to be a lifesaver for his very young Service. By 1933 the RAF was well established in the Middle East, with its Headquarters at Heliopolis near Cairo. The aircraft it was equipped with were not much different from those used in the First World War, some were by now very elderly, such as the Bristol Fighter and the DH9A. My father found himself flying the ponderous Fairey 111F (plate10) instead of the nimble little Bulldog. The Fairey 111 series of land and floatplanes served in the RAF and in several other countries' air forces. It saw brief wartime service in 1918 and was simply constructed, tough and reliable.

Easily convertible from landplane to floatplane, it is particularly remembered for its many long distance proving flights undertaken in the 1920s in the Middle East and Africa. It carried two passengers, had a maximum speed of about 120 mph and an endurance of four and a half hours. Powered by a Napier Lion engine, it was apparently so strongly built that it was difficult for even the most ham-fisted pilot to damage it, thus it was an ideal general purpose aircraft in the rough, hot, unsophisticated environment of the Middle East. At this time small, comfortable, twin engine executive types of aircraft had not been developed to transport VIPs around, so it seemed to be the logical vehicle for the AOC RAF Middle East Air Force to travel about his extended parish, despite its open cockpits and lack of creature comforts. Travel by surface means would have taken infinitely longer, been much more uncomfortable and run the risks of getting lost in the desert, mechanical breakdown and attack by the dissident tribesmen.

On the 17th of June 1933 the AOC was obviously out and about in his Command, which extended a considerable distance south of Egypt into the Sudan. Fairey IIIF J9155 appears to have been his personal aircraft. It must have been a long, hot day, with four separate flights totaling 5hours 45 minutes in all, although two flights were clearly very short hops. The Fairey IIIF had no navigation aids such as a modern aircraft would have, relying solely on an unreliable map and a magnetic compass. At least a road and railway ran south from Wadi Halfa, across the Nubian Desert. Halfway to Khartoum they join the Nile and follow it south to Khartoum; Atbara and Ed Darmer were two small settlements on the Nile 200 miles north of Khartoum in the Baiyuda Desert. Clearly there must have been some form of RAF presence at each location to warrant a visit from the AOC, even if only for refuelling. As well as navigating his precious cargo over some very desolate and inhospitable terrain – at least there was a road of sorts, a railway and the Nile to follow - my father would have had to attend all the AOC's appointments at each stop, take appropriate notes and ensure each visit proceeded smoothly (plate 11). In addition, he would have had to ensure that Fairey IIIF J9155's turn around and refueling was properly carried out; a forced landing in the Nubian Desert en route back to Wadi Halfa would not have improved his career aspirations. Today Atbara and Ed Darmer now appear to be medium size towns in Sudan; a photograph exists on the Atbara Internet site of an 'English house', there are also images of rusting steam engines dating from almost certainly the years between the First and Second World Wars. All in all, the role of ADC in this unusual environment was without doubt a challenging appointment for a young officer. Nevertheless, there must have been time for leisure activities. It would seem from the few photographs in his album that he met in Egypt a young lady who one day would be his future wife, a Miss Janet Norton, who was visiting friends and relations who were serving with the army in Egypt. It turned out to be a long courtship as their marriage took place seven years later in October 1940 in Scotland, far from the heat, dust and flies of Egypt.

Harry Eeles flew his AOC around Egypt for the last time on New Year's Eve, 1933, finishing another long expedition south by flying from Asyut to Heliopolis in J9155. After one more short night flight, solo, on 10th January 1934, he returned to England to start a course at the Air Armament School, Eastchurch, as an armament specialist. There then followed a tour as an instructor at 5 Flying Training School, Sealand. In July 1937 Newall was appointed Chief of the Air Staff and so summonsed his ADC from the time in the Middle East to take up the role of his Personal

Assistant, in today's terms his Personal Staff Officer. My father remained in this appointment until June 1940. It must have been a really hectic time, with the inevitable build up to the Second World War; sadly, my father kept no diary or written records of his time in Whitehall.

CHAPTER SIX

THE BARREN ROCKS OF ADEN

LOGBOOK ENTRY, TOM EELES

17 May 1967
Buccaneer S2 XV155
Self/Lt Fitzgerald
Aden flypast, 55 aircraft,
45minutes

Today's reader might well wonder what on earth the British were doing in such a barren, rocky, dusty, baking hot and hostile outpost of civilization that was Aden in 1967. When the Suez Canal was opened in 1869 it enabled the steam ships of that era to avoid the long and hazardous voyage to the Far East via the Cape of Good Hope. At a stroke the British Empire in India and Malaya, Australia and New Zealand became much more accessible but there was a snag; steam ship's boilers were heated by coal fired furnaces but no ships of that era carried enough coal to keep the fires lit for a long voyage to the east. The solution was to establish a coaling station en route and Aden, at the southern end of the Red Sea, was the location chosen. Coal powered steam ships had disappeared completely by the end of the Second World War but the British presence in Aden remained. The Aden Protectorate provided Great Britain with a useful toehold in the Middle East, and for the RAF a useful airfield for aircraft transiting from Europe to Africa and the Far East. However, by the mid 1960s the British were not popular as occupiers and faced a growing insurgency from the local inhabitants, encouraged actively by the regime in Egypt. Eventually it was decided to withdraw completely from the Aden Protectorate; this would be a significant task of considerable risk, given the size of the garrison and its many dependants. The RAF had a major presence at the large military airfield of Khormaksar, with fighter ground attack, transport and maritime patrol squadrons in permanent residence. There were also a large number of army units deployed to reduce the threat from rebels and insurgents and both services had a significant number of family dependant members living in Aden.

I now found myself a member of 801 Naval Air Squadron, the first Fleet Air Arm squadron to be equipped with the Blackburn Buccaneer S2, embarked on the carrier HMS Victorious. My application to volunteer for loan service with the Fleet Air Arm had been successful and I left RAF Laarbruch in July 1966 after nearly two years on 16 Squadron. After completing the Buccaneer conversion course at RNAS Lossiemouth in the far north of Scotland I again travelled slowly for a second time by RAF Transport Command Britannia to Singapore where I joined my new squadron and aircraft carrier. Service with the Royal Navy was very different to the life I had experienced so far in the RAF. My home was now a tiny cabin, 6Q6, on HMS Victorious's sixth deck, well below the water line. There was just room for a bunk, on top of a desk that opened up, a few drawers for clothes and a tiny cupboard. The nearest ablutions were some distance away through a maze of passageways. Finding one's way around the ship's interior was a challenging navigation problem. Very little had changed below deck level since Victorious was launched and commissioned in the Second World War and it was easy to get completely lost. The carrier had a distinguished record of wartime service that included being struck a number of times by Kamikazi suicide attacks. In the 1950s she was fitted with an angled flight deck, steam catapults, high capacity arrestor wires and a modern sophisticated air defence radar system, but below the flight deck she retained the interior layout had not changed much since the day she was launched in 1939.

The Buccaneer S2, which equipped 801 NAS, was a much more capable and sophisticated aircraft than the Canberra. It was originally conceived to counter the threat posed by the Soviet Navy's Sverdelov class heavy cruisers, employing a high speed, under the radar approach followed by a toss attack profile delivering a British tactical nuclear weapon called 'Red Beard'. Why it was given this unusual identification remains a mystery. With a length of sixty-four feet and a wingspan of forty-four feet the Buccaneer was a large aircraft, which had to be able to operate from the Royal Navy's rather small aircraft carriers, posing quite a challenge to its manufacturer, the Blackburn Aircraft Company. An ingenious system whereby high pressure air from the engine compressors was blown over the wings and tailplane was incorporated, thereby reducing the minimum launch speed and final approach speed to acceptable levels. By 1967 the Buccaneer had moved on from its original role of a tactical nuclear armed strike aircraft and had been modified to deliver a wide range of conventional weapons against targets both on land and at sea, it had a good photo reconnaissance capability and could also carry an air-to-air refuelling pod, so it was by far the most important offensive aircraft in the Fleet Air Arm's inventory. Powered by two Rolls Royce Spey turbo fans, it had an excellent performance and was ideally suited to high-speed flight and air to ground weapon delivery from low altitudes.

Launching from and recovering to an aircraft carrier was an altogether far more challenging and exciting business than flying from an airfield and required the learning of new handling skills. The catapult launch involved being accelerated from zero to 130kts in a mere one hundred and forty five feet; it was a 'hands off' launch with the tail plane trim set to rotate the aircraft into the climbing attitude without any pilot input. At this low speed the Buccaneer was very sensitive to pitch inputs and any over-controlling by the pilot could lead to a stall and disaster, so it was better to let the aircraft do its own thing. Once safely in the air and accelerating the pilot would gently take control, clean up the landing gear and high lift flap and drooped ailerons and then carry on as normal. Returning to the ship was always a time of heightened tension; the ship looked impossibly small to land on and it required very accurate flying to arrive safely at the right speed and place for an arrested landing. There was really no margin for error. The learning of these new techniques seems to me to be somewhat similar to my father's experience in the 1930s on being propelled from the comfort of a home counties based fighter squadron to a new environment of working and flying with a very senior officer in Egypt.

May 1967 found HMS Victorious on her way back home after a tour of duty east of Suez. She was to be relieved by HMS Hermes and the two carriers were planned to meet off Aden. The military staffs in Aden decided that this meeting presented a once-in-a-lifetime opportunity to impress the local dissidents with a display of British potential firepower, in order to dissuade them from interfering with the forthcoming withdrawal. Therefore a mass flypast was planned to cover large areas of the Aden Protectorate, consisting of the Buccaneer and Sea Vixen squadrons embarked on the two carriers and the fighter squadrons equipped with Hunter ground attack fighters based at the RAF airfield at Khormaksar in Aden. This large formation of different aircraft types totalled some fifty-five fast jet aircraft (plate 12), a most impressive spectacle that is unlikely ever to be seen again. I was tasked to fly as the number two in a four aircraft element of Buccaneers on the right hand side of the formation. My observer was Lieutenant Jim Fitzgerald, an Irishman with strong republican sympathies and not my usual observer but an entertaining character nonetheless. Victorious succeeded in launching eight of our nine Buccaneers and eight Sea Vixens, plus a couple of 'planeguard' Wessex helicopters, no mean feat at this stage of the commission when the aircraft were all in need of some shore-based long term maintainence. We joined up with our Buccaneer and Sea Vixen colleagues from Hermes. The RAF at Khormaksar contributed twenty-seven Hunters which joined the Fleet Air Arm contingent. A 'larger than life' character called Pete Shepherd, flying in a Sea Vixen from Hermes, led this huge formation once all its elements had joined up. He didn't seem to worry too much about abrupt changes of heading and speed, so as a consequence the whiplash effect on the Hunters at the back of the formation was considerable. It was very much a case of hanging on to the leader of your element as best you could, whilst ignoring the plaintive cries from the rear elements of this 'Balbo'[1]. As can be imagined, it was hot work.

Meanwhile, down on the surface of the Gulf of Aden, the Royal Navy made best use of the equally rare opportunity of operating two aircraft carriers together (plate 13). This maritime activity was really of no interest to us busy aircrew until it was time to recover on board. We found the two aircraft carriers steaming in line abreast about three miles apart. The wind was fairly light but from a consistent direction. Both carriers headed so as to put the wind directly down their angled flight decks, but unfortunately no one had realized that the angle of Hermes's flight deck was different to Victorious, consequently both ships slowly converged during the rather protracted landing-on sequence. The landing circuits became somewhat confused to the extent that you had to make sure you were about to 'hook on' to the right carrier. Luckily Victorious had a large fluorescent red letter V painted on her flight deck (plate 14). Once all aircraft had finally landed the two carriers anchored off Steamer Point in the harbour at Aden. The ambient sea temperature was so high that the ship's air conditioning system could not work properly, so the flight deck was flooded with water in an attempt to cool the interior. All this resulted in producing was exceptionally warm fog below decks.

---

[1] Balbo – a large formation of aircraft, named after the Italian General Balbo who flew a large formation across the Atlantic in the 1920s.

We gratefully accepted the Hunter squadrons' invitation to a party in the Officers' Mess ashore where the air conditioning did work.

We travelled from the landing stage to the Officers' Mess in a bus that had its glass windows replaced by wire mesh to prevent stones or grenades being thrown in by the locals, guarded by a soldier in the bus's door with a sub machine gun. The following evening, when the temperature had dropped somewhat, HMS Victorious hosted a return party for the Hunter pilots before leaving early next morning for the Suez Canal. There was some doubt as to whether a passage of the Canal would be permitted owing to the rapidly deteriorating situation between Israel and the Arab nations but in the event we passed through, only to be held in the Mediterranean awaiting the outcome of the Middle East crisis. The carrier spent the whole of the subsequent Six Day Arab/Israeli War in Grand Harbour, Malta, before finally returning to Portsmouth somewhat later than originally intended. Victorious never went to sea again, suffering superficial damage from a fire on board during dockyard re-fit work and a subsequent political decision not to repair her. I remained a member of 801 Squadron until the summer of 1968, when the squadron was re-assigned to HMS Hermes and reduced in strength from nine to six aircraft prior to embarking, as Hermes was a smaller ship than Victorious. My time on loan to the Royal Navy came to an end, but not my association with the Buccaneer, as will be described in Chapter Eight.

CHAPTER SEVEN

AN INSTRUCTIONAL INTERLUDE

LOGBOOK ENTRY, HARRY EELES

23 March 1937
Hart K4939
Self/Acting Pilot Officer Shore
Air to Ground firing
30 minutes

In February 1934 Harry Eeles returned to England from Egypt, travelling in a flying boat across the Mediterranean Sea at a sedate pace with night stops at suitable hotels en route. In those days RAF general duties officers were expected to acquire some form of specialization in addition to their qualification as a pilot, so my father opted to become an air armament specialist, the 1930s equivalent of what in today's RAF would be called a Qualified Weapons Instructor. He undertook the air armament course at RAF Eastchurch at the Air Armament School from March 1934 to January 1935. Whilst on the course he flew two new types of aircraft, the Westland Wapiti and the Hawker Hart, and renewed his association with the Bristol Bulldog. He completed the course with an assessment of Above the Average and was posted as an instructor to No 5 Flying Training School at RAF Sealand in Cheshire.

In the early 1930s the realization slowly began to dawn in Great Britain that rearmament and modernization of the armed forces, particularly the RAF, which had been neglected for many years after the end of the First World War, was now inevitable. In Germany and Italy the rise of the dictators Hitler and Mussolini with their firebrand creeds of National Socialism and Fascism did not auger well for continued peace in Europe. Despite the

Government's policy of appeasement when dealing with these dictators, the RAF's Expansion Plan A was started in February 1934, along with a major review of the arrangements for flying training. This review recommended that the Flying Training Schools should provide a ten month long course divided into two terms of five months. The first term would concentrate on pure flying skills on service aircraft types, the students having previously completed an ab-initio course at a civil flying school. The second term would introduce applied flying in the form of instrument flying, navigation, air gunnery and bombing. Expansion Plan B was rapidly overtaken by Plan C, which in May 1935, amongst other things established the student strength of eighty per course at the Flying Training Schools.

At the same time many new airfields began to be constructed, with their buildings having a distinctive neo-Georgian style of architecture, which still can be seen at a number of RAF airfields today. The aircraft industry was starting to develop a new generation of fast monoplane combat aircraft by way of a response to what was happening in Germany, but the RAF's aircraft in service were still lagging well behind these developments. In the summer of 1935 a Royal Review of the RAF took place at RAF Mildenhall and Duxford. The programme for this event (plate15) has a front cover which optimistacly shows a proud lion standing aggressively on top of a large puffy cumulus cloud floating over England, the epitome of military confidence. However, perusal of the programme's contents reveals that all three hundred and fifty six aircraft of the thirty-seven squadrons on parade were biplanes. Thus the situation that my father would have experienced on arrival at 5 Flying Training School, RAF Sealand, was one of a painfully slow expansion of RAF facilities, personnel and equipment, set against a background of an increasingly deteriorating state of international affairs in the world outside the RAF.

Harry Eeles spent two years and five months as an instructor at Sealand, his longest tour of duty so far. Whilst there he flew no fewer than seven different aircraft types, the Armstrong Whitworth Atlas, Fairey Gordon, Avro Tutor, the Hawker Tomtit, Audax, Hart and Fury. This is a strange mix of types, all biplanes, but all typical of the rather muddled style of RAF flying training equipment in the 1930s. The Tutor and Tomtit were basic trainers, the Atlas, Gordon and Hart were general-purpose light bombers, the Audax was an army co-operation aircraft and the Fury was the first fighter in the RAF to exceed 200 mph, but not by much. The Hawker Aircraft Company produced a series of good-looking biplanes in the late 1920s and early 1930s, which undertook a number of different roles. The Hart and Hind were light bombers, the Hardy was a general-purpose aircraft and the Audax was a specialized army co-operation aircraft developed from the Hart. The Demon was a two-seat fighter, the Fury a fast single seat fighter and the Osprey and Nimrod were navalised versions of the Demon and Fury. They all looked very similar and were all powered by the Rolls Royce Kestrel liquid cooled V12 aero engine driving a two blade fixed pitch propellor. The Hart (plate 16) had a wingspan of thirty-seven feet and a maximum speed of 184 mph. It entered RAF service in January 1930 and proved to be a popular and capable aircraft; many lingered on as advanced trainers well into the 1940s. One is still flown regularly today with the Shuttleworth Collection, Old Warden, and an example can be seen in the RAF Museum at Hendon.

The flight chosen for this chapter was an air to ground firing sortie in Hart K4939. There is no detail in the logbook entry as to where this took place but it must have been on an air weapons range. The Hart had a single forward firing machine gun recessed in the left side of the fuselage and a single machine gun mounted on a scarf ring on the edge of the rear cockpit. My guess is that this flight involved using only the forward firing gun, as the student was an Acting Pilot Officer. He must have been a pilot under training as air gunners in the 1930s were recruited from the non-commissioned ranks. The flight was quite short at only 30 minutes. The Hart was evidently a delightful aircraft to fly; when it entered service in 1930 it could outpace any of the RAF's fighters, giving further credence to the concept popular at the time that 'The bomber will always get through'.

The following extract from Group Captain Frank Tredrey's wonderful book 'A Pilot's Summer' is a classic description of biplane handling characteristics and will give the reader an idea of what a Hawker Hart was like to fly. *'She has a tendency to swing to the left as you take off, which has to be firmly counteracted with right rudder; and you can see a frightful lot of ground ahead over the tapered nose when you're in flying position......climb seems rather steep after Tutors because she's so much more powerful......straight and level flight, once more you can see a lot of ground ahead, and until you've watched the altimeter for a time and noticed that it doesn't register a change, could swear that you're diving her......turns very nice, with a Hart you can rip into a turn and out again as smoothly as slipping down a water-shoot.......spinning nice and slow. Needs full opposite rudder to make her come out. Aerobatics? Far easier than Avro 504N, Tutor or Atlas. Plenty of loading in rolls off a loop.....Landings a little bit tricky. On a windy day you have to get the stick back that last little bit in double quick time or else she drops on to a nice springy undercarriage and goes up like a lift to about five feet, half bouncing and half ballooning with the wind under the wings....give her a touch of throttle as she sinks, she'll stay down all right the second time....I gave her a good fat burst and she sat down like a two year old.'*

The flying at 5 Flying Training School must have been somewhat repetitive and boring by its very nature, especially when compared to that experienced on a fighter squadron or as the AOC's personal pilot in the Middle East. Nevertheless, the chance to fly such beautiful aircraft as the Hart, Audax and Fury must have been a considerable compensation for the routine nature of the training task, representing as they did the peak of military biplane design and performance. There are a number of short flights in the Fury recorded in Harry Eeles's logbook of just aerobatics. The Fury must have been the ultimate biplane fighter, but it was out of date by the mid 1930s. Hawker's new fighter, the monoplane Hurricane, first flew on 6th November 1935. With its Merlin engine of 1000hp, a retractable undercarriage, enclosed cockpit, armament of eight machine guns and a top speed of over 300mph it was a huge advance on aircraft such as the Hart and Fury. There would be no going back now to glamorous open cockpit silver biplanes.

Harry Eeles left 5 Flying Training School at the end of July 1937 with an assessment of 'Above the Average as a Light Bomber pilot'. After a short spell of leave, sailing with his elder brother Tristram Eeles in their yacht on the Norfolk Broads, he moved to London to take up the appointment of Personal Assistant to the Chief of Air Staff. His service in Egypt had obviously been well received, as his old AOC from the Middle East, Cyril Newall, was now Air Chief Marshal Sir Cyril Newall, appointed as Chief of the Air Staff on 1st September 1937. The next two and a half years would have been utterly fascinating as the Munich Crisis and the build up to and outbreak of the Second World War took place. Harry Eeles must have been aware of the highest level of diplomatic, political and military planning and decisions taken in those two and a half years. It was an era of appeasement of the dictators but continued expansion of the RAF. Sadly he kept no diary or record of that period and we next meet him back in the cockpit in Chapter 9.

CHAPTER EIGHT

INSTRUCTING THIRTY-TWO YEARS LATER

LOGBOOK ENTRY, TOM EELES

14 March 1969
Gnat T1 XS107
Self/Flying Officer Brady
Exercise 7, maximum rate turns
1.00 hour

The period between 1967 and 1969 was one of turbulence and uncertainty in both the RAF and RN. In 1965 one of the incoming Labour administration's first actions was to cancel the RAF's projected replacement for the Canberra, the TSR2, at the same time withdrawing the nation from its defence commitments east of Suez and cancelling the future aircraft carrier programme, CVA01. The RAF was promised a replacement for TSR2 in the form of a purchase from the USA of the F111 strike aircraft but it was not long before this was also cancelled. An Anglo French proposal for a joint variable geometry aircraft never made any progress. After further debate the Government eventually decided that the RAF would take over the Fleet Air Arm's newly arrived Phantoms, when the remaining aircraft carriers were decommissioned. A further order for Phantoms was made. The Fleet Air Arm's Buccaneers would also be passed to the RAF as a short-term 'stop gap' replacement for the TSR2 and more were also ordered from the manufacturer Hawker Siddeley, this firm having absorbed the Blackburn Aircraft Company.

Meanwhile a joint Anglo/German/Italian project to build a new multi-role combat aircraft would be initiated, which ultimately became the Tornado. All this took place whilst I was still on loan to the Fleet Air Arm, when my squadron was re-assigned from

HMS Victorious to HMS Hermes. Victorious suffered a fire whilst in dry dock and was subsequently not re-commissioned. Hermes was smaller than Victorious so the squadron was reduced from nine to six aircraft and consequently my services on loan were no longer needed. I was summonsed to MoD and informed that I would be sent to the Central Flying School to be trained as a flying instructor, then, after a few months gaining some instructional experience on the Folland Gnat advanced trainer at RAF Valley, I would return to the Buccaneer training squadron, 736 NAS, at RNAS Lossiemouth. The RN had agreed that it would provide the first two years of Buccaneer conversion training for the RAF, provided the instructional strength of 736 NAS was bolstered by the addition of some the RAF pilots and navigators who had flown the Buccaneer with the Fleet Air Arm. I was to be one of them. What I was not told was that the Mk1 version of the Buccaneer, with its low thrust unreliable Gyron Junior engines, was to be brought out of retirement for the RAF training task.

I joined the CFS instructor course in August 1968 as a student, and, unlike anyone else on the course, I knew exactly where I was going to go at the end of the course, provided I passed. The course finished in December and in January 1969 I drove from Little Rissington to Anglesey and joined 2 Squadron, 4 FTS, RAF Valley as a newly qualified Gnat flying instructor, expecting to be there for about five months. Unsurprisingly, the 4 FTS hierarchy were quite unaware of the very short time I was expecting to be with them and protests were made about why I had taken up one of the only two Gnat slots for RAF pilots on the CFS course, only to move on so soon. Nevertheless, despite these complaints, the plan remained unchanged. I was assigned to the refresher flight on 2 Squadron that was tasked with giving refresher flying to pilots who had already graduated from Valley but were waiting for further courses at Operational Conversion Units, there being a considerable backlog in the training pipeline caused by all the reductions and changes in RAF front line equipment outlined above.

The Folland Gnat (plate 17) was another aircraft designed by W E Petter. He was also the designer of the Westland Whirlwind fighter (see Chapter 9), the Canberra (see Chapter 4) and the English Electric P1 research aircraft, which was subsequently developed into the Lightning fighter. Petter left the Westland Aircraft Company in 1946 and joined English Electric, where he was responsible for the design of the very successful Canberra light bomber. Later, whilst working on the P1 project at English Electric, Petter became disillusioned with the seemingly inexorable rise in the size, complexity and cost of fighter aircraft. He left English Electric and joined the Folland Aircraft Company, where he started work on a small, lightweight fighter that he hoped would reverse the trend of increasing size and cost. The final result was the Gnat, a tiny, elegant aircraft powered by an Orpheus turbo-jet engine, armed with two 30mm cannon. It had a sparkling performance and was offered to the RAF as a possible replacement for the Venom ground attack fighter but it was rejected in favour of the more robust and simpler Hunter. A small number were exported to Finland and Yugoslavia and considerably more to India, where it was built in large numbers under licence as the Ajeet.

A two-seat trainer version, without armament but with increased fuel capacity, was offered to the RAF as a replacement for the Vampire advanced trainer. It had a transonic performance, being capable of exceeding Mach 1.0 in a shallow dive; to quote Pilots' Notes, 'well-contoured airframes in steep dives approach Mach 1.3.' It was equipped with the advanced Integrated Flight Instrument System (IFIS) (plate18) that was also fitted in the Lightning and Buccaneer and had been planned for the TSR2, thus it represented a very significant advance on the Vampire. It was very small, with a wingspan of just twenty-four feet, it was thirty-

Plate 1 IMGavro504_0003 – The Lynx powered Avro 504, WW1 veteran and mainstay of the RAF's training fleet, 1918 – 1931

Plate 2 IMGcw1929 – The Senior Entry, RAF College Cranwell, 1930. Harry Eeles seated front row centre.

Plate 3 IMGbike – Harry Eeles shows off his issue motorbike to his elder brother and younger step-brother, Wavendon House, 1930.

Plate 4 IMGcwchip-0002 – A Cranwell based Chipmunk showing Cranwell's blue band round the fuselage.

Plate 5 Large(1) – The Jet Provost flight line at Cranwell, 1962. Note the dress code, the cadets are all wearing ties with flying suits, very formal.

Plate 6 IMG_0003 – A Bulldog formation.

Plate 7 IMG_0001 – Bulldogs under construction, Filton. K2190 was Harry Eeles's personal aircraft.

Plate 8 Canberra0020 – Two Canberras getting airborne from Kuantan.

Plate 9 IMGkuantan – The Officers' Mess marquee, Kuantan.

Plate 10 IMGfairey3f – A Fairey 111F, the AOC's transport in 1930s Middle East.

Plate 11 IMGegypt_0003 – Air Vice Marshal Cyril Newall and a group of RAF officers in the desert. Harry Eeles hovers anxiously in the background.

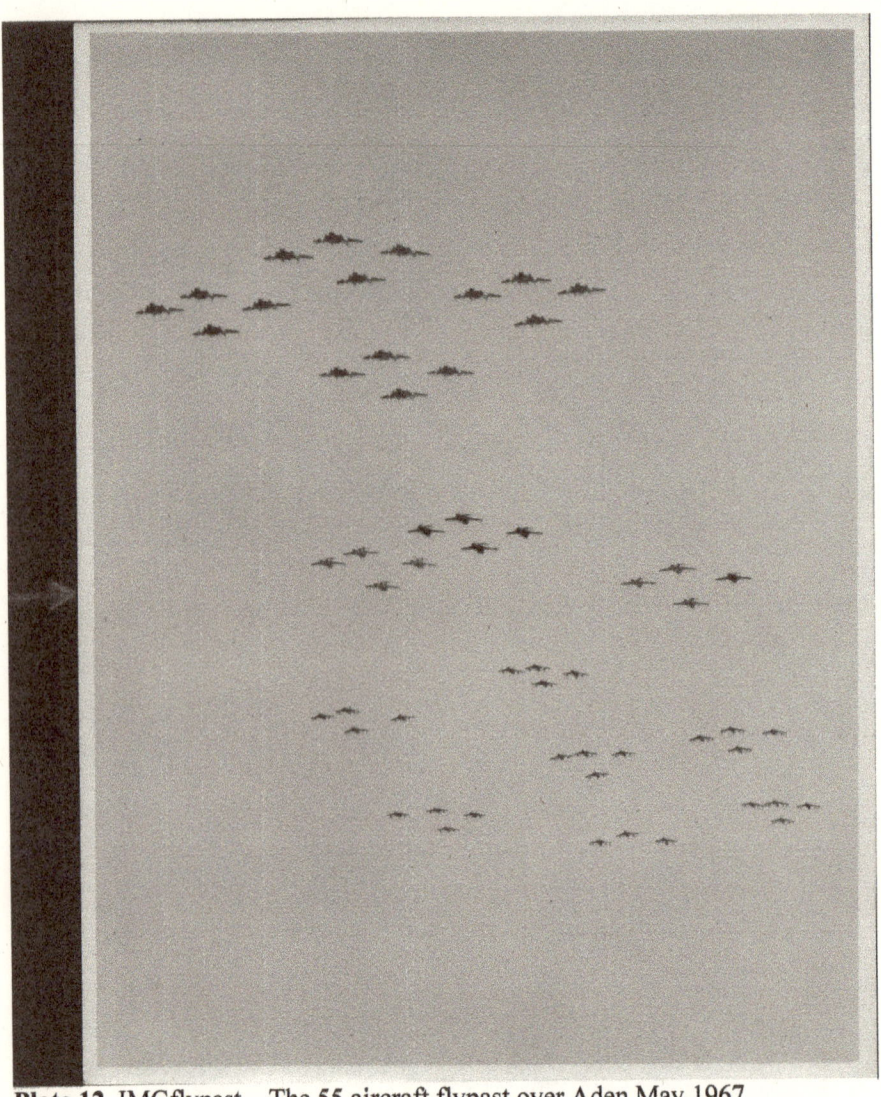

Plate 12 IMGflypast – The 55 aircraft flypast over Aden May 1967.

Plate 13 Buccaneer0010 – HMS Victorious and Hermes await the return of their aircraft, Aden, May 1967.

Plate 14 IMGvicaden – Overhead view of HMS Victorious after recovering Sea Vixens and Buccaneers, Aden, May 1967.

Plate 15 IMG1935review – The cover of the programme for the Royal Review of the RAF, 1935.

Plate 16 IMGharts – An advertisement for Rolls Royce aero engines showing the ubiquitous Hawker Hart, 1935.

Plate 17 08GNATS(2) – A line up of Gnats at RAF Valley, 1969.

Plate 18 CFS0013 – The Gnat's complicated flight instrument panel.

Plate 19 Whirlwind3 – Westland Whirlwind F1, P6966, the first production aircraft, delivered to 263 Sqn by Harry Eeles, 7 July 1940.

Plate 20 Whirlwind7 – 263 Squadron personnel, July 1940. Harry Eeles in centre with pipe and swagger stick.

Plate 21 IMGwedding1940 – Harry Eeles's wedding party, South Queensferry, 22 October 1940.

Plate 22 IMGhunter – A Hunter FGA9 over a Russian Kresta 1 light cruiser, Alboran anchorage.

Plate 23 IMGGibrw – The view of Gibraltar's easterly runway. The Rock is just out of view to the right, Spain to the left.

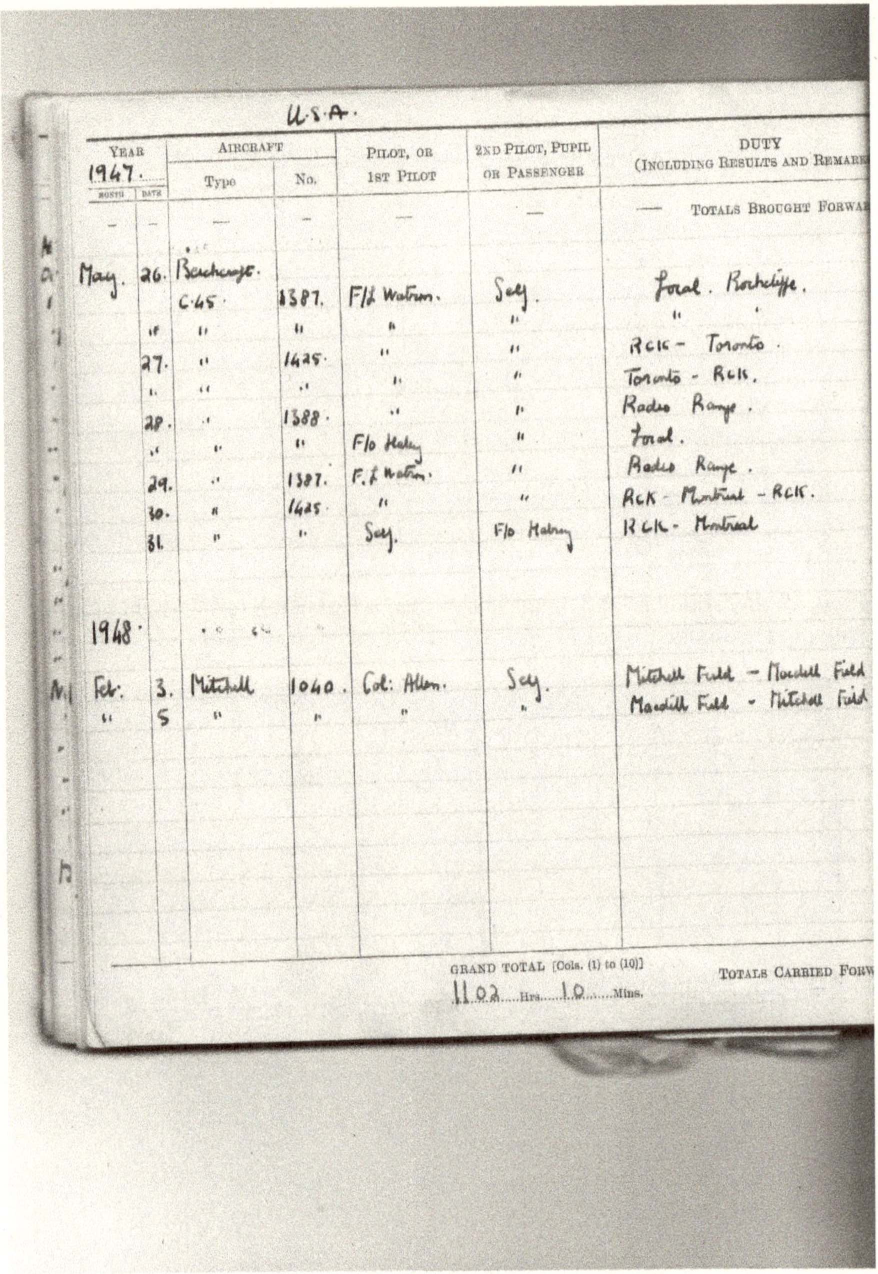

U.S.A.

YEAR 1947		AIRCRAFT		PILOT, OR 1ST PILOT	2ND PILOT, PUPIL OR PASSENGER	DUTY (INCLUDING RESULTS AND REMARKS)
MONTH	DATE	Type	No.			
—	—	—	—	—	—	TOTALS BROUGHT FORWARD
May	26	Beechcraft C-45	1387	F/L Watson	Self	Local. Rockcliffe.
"	"	"	"	"	"	"
"	27	"	1425	"	"	RCK – Toronto
"	"	"	"	"	"	Toronto – RCK
"	28	"	1388	"	"	Radio Range
"	"	"	"	F/O Haley	"	Local
"	29	"	1387	F/L Watson	"	Radio Range
"	30	"	1425	"	"	RCK – Montreal – RCK
"	31	"	"	Self	F/O Haley	RCK – Montreal
1948						
Feb	3	Mitchell	1040	Col: Allen	Self	Mitchell Field – MacDill Field
"	5	"	"	"	"	MacDill Field – Mitchell Field

GRAND TOTAL [Cols. (1) to (10)]
1102 Hrs. 10 Mins.

TOTALS CARRIED FORWARD

Plate 24 IMGlogbook – The Canadian refresher logbook entries.

Plate 25 The Beechcraft C 45

Plate 26 IMGjetstream 0005 – The Jetstream, the last Handley Page aircraft to serve in the RAF.

Plate 27 IMGjetstream0006 – Working in the Jetstream's flight deck.

Plate 28 IMGvampire – The Vampire F1, an excellent mount for an air race.

Plate 29 Eeles Meteor12 – Watching the air race, RAF Thorney Island Battle of Britain Day, 1949.

Plate 30 IMGredarrows – The Red Arrows, the RAF Aerobatic Team.

Plate 31 IMGexamwg – Examining Wing, known as The 'Trappers', with their aircraft, CFS, RAF Scampton 1989.

Plate 32 Legends005 – A typical scene at the Flying Legends Airshow, Duxford.

Plate 33 IMGcmdtcw – Air Commodore Harry Eeles Commandant and AOC, RAF College Cranwell, 1952–1956.

Plate 34 IMGballiol13_0003 – The Balliol T2, something of an anachronism in the jet age.

Plate 35 IMGballiol_0004 – A Balliol T2 over the RAF College.

Plate 36 IMGocloo – Group Captain Tom Eeles Officer Commanding RAF Linton on Ouse and No1 Flying Training School, 1992 – 1994.

Plate 37 07a2jp5 – The Jet Provost T5A, workhorse of the RAF's flying training system, 1965 –1994.

Plate 38 IMGanson_0003 – Avro Anson light transport, Harry Eeles's last service aircraft.

Plate 39 31Tutor(2) – Grob 115E Tutor elementary trainer, Tom Eeles's last service aircraft.

Plate 40 IMG_000(5) – A glass of champagne at the end – Tom Eeles, No 5 Air Experience Flight, RAF Wyton, 28 June 2010.

seven feet long and the height of the fin was just ten feet, so not much bigger than the Chipmunk. However, technically it was not a simple aircraft like its contemporary the Hunter. The longitudinal control system was particularly complicated, the landing gear doubled up as an airbrake when partially extended and its small size meant that tall pilots could not fit in it. Many people wondered why the two seat version of the Hunter had not been selected as the Vampire's replacement, especially as it had side by side seating (the RAF's favoured layout) like the Jet Provost, was still in production, was available in large numbers and was considerably more robust and serviceable than the Gnat. Rumour had it that Follands claimed that the IFIS could not be fitted in a Hunter and that IFIS was an essential requirement for a new advanced trainer; this was nonsense as the RN and RAF both had two seat Hunters fitted with the IFIS. Much more likely was the fact that an influential retired Air Marshal was on the Board of Directors at Folland and the order for Gnat trainers was something of a consolation prize for losing the ground attack aircraft competition.

Ironically, an additional squadron using both two and single seat Hunters soon had to be formed at Valley to undertake advanced flying training for pilots too tall to fit in the Gnat, for overseas customers who found the Gnat too complicated to cope with and to cater for lack of Gnat availability due to its high level of unserviceability. The Gnat had entered service at Valley as a trainer in 1962 and by 1969, when I arrived as an instructor, was suffering from poor availability due to many technical issues. By way of an example, there was an occasion when the RN exchange officer and I took a Gnat away for the day to Lossiemouth to enable him to do some naval admin. Whilst waiting for him I took another naval officer flying to show him the Gnat's performance. We had only been airborne a few minutes when we were told by ATC to return and land as soon as possible, using minimum control inputs. After landing I was informed that during a Gnat's post servicing maintenance test flight that morning the aileron control cables had snapped, which resulted in the whole fleet being grounded. It was going to take quite a time to return the fleet to a serviceable state so there was no other option than to return by train to Valley, still clad in our immersion suits and clutching our flying helmets and lifejackets. Two small boys on Crewe railway station asked us if we were astronauts!

However, when it was serviceable the Gnat was a delight to fly, especially from the front seat. It was so small that it felt like you put the aircraft on like an item of clothing rather than climbing in. With its long pitot tube sticking out ahead flying it from the front seat was often compared to riding a witch's broomstick. It had good acceleration, a very high rate of roll and the controls were wonderfully light and harmonized when in power; in manual, after a hydraulic failure, it was a different story altogether. It had a hydraulic on/off selector, which allowed the instructor to put the controls into manual. Many hours were spent struggling to fly the Gnat in this condition, particularly if associated with a practice engine failure. Needless to say, the hydraulic system and the engine were generally the most reliable systems in the Gnat. The instructor sat in the rear seat from which the view ahead consisted of the student's ejection seat and flying helmet. The rear seat flight instruments were scattered around in a rather random fashion with a quite different layout from the front seat. The view ahead from the rear seat on final approach, particularly if doing a flapless landing, was appalling by day and even worse at night, when there were multiple reflections from the runway lights on the canopy.

A small airspeed indicator which showed airspeeds between 100 and 200 kts was provided on the rear cockpit left coaming to give an accurate 'head out' airspeed indication in the circuit for the instructor, who would therefore hope for a cross wind from the right. The Gnat's narrow track landing gear made cross wind operations tricky, the limitation on take off and landing on a dry runway being 20kts, reducing to 10kts on a wet runway.

Perversely, the westerly runway at Valley, which was aligned with the prevailing wind, was considered too short for normal Gnat operations. The Gnat had no internal starter system so relied on an external gas turbine starter trolley for engine starting, thus somewhat limiting the choice of other airfields to visit. Despite all these idiosyncratic characteristics and its chronic unserviceability we all loved flying the Gnat.

The sortie chosen for this chapter consisted of teaching the student how to achieve and maintain the maximum possible rate of turn, an essential skill for any budding fighter pilot. The instructor would first demonstrate the maximum rate of turn achievable in level flight, starting at a speed of around 360 – 400 kts. The entry technique was to apply full power, roll the aircraft to the maximum angle of bank and to pull back to achieve the aircraft's 'g' limit. However, the Gnat did not have enough thrust from its Orpheus turbo jet at full power to maintain a level maximum rate turn at the maximum permitted 'g' value; the speed would reduce and the onset of pre stall buffet would soon become the limiting factor. The pre stall, or light buffet, thus imposed a limit on turning performance, as to tighten the turn further would result in heavy buffet, a large reduction in rate of turn and possible loss of control. A level turn in this condition could now only be maintained by varying the angle of bank; if climbing, increase bank angle, if descending, reduce it, whilst maintaining the light buffet. Once the student had mastered the technique of maintaining a maximum rate level turn on the light buffet, the instructor would observe that the turn rate was not particularly impressive, limited as it was by the inability to tighten the turn by pulling more 'g'. The 'g' value sustained in a maximum rate level turn would be well below the Gnat's permitted maximum of 7g.

So how could turning performance be improved to achieve the maximum possible rate of turn? The answer was to overbank the aircraft and allow it to descend and accelerate, whilst maintaining full power and the light buffet. As the aircraft gained speed an increasingly higher 'g' value could be achieved, until eventually the light buffet and max permitted 'g' coincided, thus producing the maximum possible rate of turn. The penalty of course was a significant loss of height. This exercise was physically exhausting for both instructor and student. Much of it was spent at high 'g' values, which required considerable physical effort to counteract, assisted by the inflation around legs and stomach of the anti 'g' suit. Speaking lucidly under high 'g' was difficult for the instructor. At 6 'g', the usual maximum used on this exercise, the human head wearing a bulky flying helmet weighs six times its normal weight. Move your head inadvertently and you could suffer severe neck muscle pain or injury. Relax and 'g' induced loss of consciousness could occur. After completing this exercise the flight would usually conclude with some aerobatics, some form of practice emergency and either an instrument or visual recovery to Valley. The Gnat was well equipped for instrument recoveries, with TACAN as a navigation aid with an offset facility, ILS and a Zero Reader for precision approaches. The IFIS's display of these aids was excellent.

In addition to its role as an advanced trainer the Gnat's main claim to fame was as the chosen mount of the Red Arrows, the RAF's aerobatic team. The introduction of the Lightning and Javelin as the RAF's main interceptor fighters resulted in the cost of forming aerobatic teams from front line squadrons becoming prohibitively expensive. Neither aircraft was really suitable for formation display flying and the only other possibility, the Hunter, was now considered to be too old. In the early 1960s some of the flying instructors at Valley who had previously been members of the Black Arrows display team decided to form a team using the Gnat. They had the aircraft painted yellow and called themselves the Yellow Jacks. The Gnat proved to be an ideal display aircraft with its great manoeuvrability, spectacular rate of roll, small size and relatively low cost of operation. However, higher authority did not like the name Yellow Jacks so the team were renamed the Red Arrows, moved from Valley to Kemble where they became part of the Central Flying School establishment and so became the official RAF Aerobatic Display Team. Formed initially with seven aircraft they soon expanded to the universally recognized nine and under the initial leadership of Squadron Leader Ray Hanna rapidly established themselves as the world's premier formation aerobatic display team. They flew the Gnat from 1965 until the end of 1979, by which time the Gnat had been replaced as a trainer by the Hawk at Valley, so they too exchanged their Gnats for the Hawk. But this was not quite the end of the Gnat story.

After being retired from flying duties a number of Gnat airframes were used at the engineer training school at RAF Cosford to train ground crew in turn round operations. The aircraft systems and engines were maintained in an airworthy condition and used regularly. Eventually, when finally surplus to the RAF's needs, they were sold. Some were bought by private civilian owners, who placed them on the civil register with the intention of flying them at air displays. However, keeping a complex fast jet aircraft like the Gnat in working order more than 35 years after it was taken out of RAF service is a very challenging proposition for both pilots and technical support staff. Maintaining an adequate level of piloting skill and currency is also a very expensive business when each flight probably costs considerably more than £1000. RAF display pilots fly the aircraft they display almost every day as part of their job, averaging 10 to 20 hours a month; a civilian pilot flying a civilian registered Gnat would be lucky to get twenty hours a year. I have serious misgivings about the viability of flying 1960s vintage fast jet aircraft, particularly those as complex and unforgiving as the Gnat, on the air display circuit by civilian pilots with little or no military flying experience, a private pilot's licence and such a small amount of flying.

After nearly five months on 2 squadron's refresher flight my time as a Gnat instructor came to an end. The prospect of remaining at Valley was tempting, as I much enjoyed the aircraft and the role, however, I returned to RNAS Lossiemouth and joined 736 Naval Air Squadron as a Qualified Flying Instructor. My role now was to sit in the rear seat of the Buccaneer on the student pilot's first flight. There were no flying or engine controls and only very limited navigational instruments in the rear seat, so a convincing line of instructional 'patter' was essential to ensure the flight's successful conclusion. This was an altogether different prospect when compared to teaching on the Gnat, although the view from the rear seat of the Buccaneer was quite good. I soon developed the necessary convincing line of instructional 'patter'. At least we had some two seat Hunters, which enabled the instructors to get a feel for a student's handling skills before sending him off for his first flight in a Buccaneer.

One of these first flights in a Buccaneer Mk1 ended in disaster, when the left engine failed at a critical point on an overshoot from an approach. The Buccaneer now had insufficient thrust to continue flying so we both ejected, in full view of the squadron. Despite seriously damaging my back I continued instructing after a three month lay off. In the event I ended up doing no fewer than four instructional tours on the Buccaneer, finally ending up as the Commanding Officer of the Buccaneer Operational Conversion Unit. However, my experience as a QFI expanded to include elementary, basic, advanced, tactical weapons and examining skills, so that CFS course in 1968 could be argued to have been money well spent.

CHAPTER NINE

THE SECOND WORLD WAR

LOGBOOK ENTRY, HARRY EELES

7 July 1940
Whirlwind F 1 P6966
Self
Dishforth to Drem, Drem to Grangemouth.
Delivery to 263 Squadron.
1.00 hour, 15 minutes.

As the 1930s progressed some armament specialists in the Air Ministry became increasingly concerned about the ability of the RAF's slow biplane fighters, armed with two machine guns firing rifle caliber .303 ammunition, to shoot down the new generation of fast, heavily armed bombers being developed in Germany and Italy. Even the prospect of the fast monoplane fighters armed with eight machine guns, being developed by Hawkers and Supermarine, seemed unlikely to offer a complete solution. A new more powerful gun was needed, along with a much faster fighter capable of carrying it.

Eventually a suitable gun was found, the Hispano-Suiza 20mm cannon, originally developed in France but able to be manufactured under licence in England. In 1935 the Air Ministry issued an invitation to the aircraft manufacturing industry, F37/35, to tender for a single seat day and night fighter, to be cannon armed, with a speed in excess of a contemporary bomber of at least 40 mph at 15,000ft. Westland, a small West Country aircraft manufacturer located in Yeovil, submitted a proposal by its Chief Designer W E Petter for a twin - engine single seat fighter powered by two Rolls Royce Peregrine engines, with a battery of four

20mm cannon installed in the nose. As most of the other submissions for this tender were from manufacturers with little spare capacity to develop a new design, Westland were awarded the contract, somewhat to the surprise of the rest of the aircraft industry and the RAF, given Westland's lack of experience in the design and manufacture of high speed fighter aircraft.

The first prototype, soon to be named Whirlwind, flew in late 1938. It was a very advanced design for that period, with a 'bubble' canopy affording a superb view for the pilot, a complex radiator system inside the wing linked to the flaps which did away with the need for external high drag radiators, a high set tail plane and a fully retractable landing gear which included the tail wheel. It was a very good-looking fighter, small and fast, faster even than the early Spitfires and considerably faster than the Hurricane, and very heavily armed. It was designed as a bomber destroyer rather than an air combat fighter, as the notion that enemy fighters from Germany might be met over England in air combat was considered extremely unlikely in 1938.

No one had thought that the collapse of France, with the largest army in Europe, would ever happen in the spectacularly quick fashion that it did some two years later. The Whirlwind's advanced design and complex stressed metal construction proved very challenging for Westland, whose previous manufacturing experience had been limited mainly to simple fabric covered aircraft. Early trials revealed a number of problems. Petter, in his attempt to produce the most streamlined airframe, had routed the engine exhausts through the inside of the wing to discharge from the trailing edge. Unsurprisingly, on an early test flight the aileron control run was burnt through and Westland's test pilot with great skill managed to land the precious prototype successfully. Redesign was necessary. Thus the first production aircraft were only just starting to appear by early 1940. Meanwhile, during this somewhat protracted development, considerable debate had taken place within the Air Ministry staffs about the future of the Whirlwind. In the spring of 1939 the Cabinet set the Army the goal of creating a Field Force of no less than thirty-two divisions rather than nine. Subsequent RAF estimates concluded that this new massively expanded Field Force would need thirteen additional squadrons of army co-operation aircraft.

The only army co-operation aircraft available at that time was the Lysander, also manufactured by Westland. These new army co-operation squadrons would need two hundred and thirty four aircraft; losses in intensive war operations were calculated to be as many as one hundred and sixty three aircraft a month and Westland were only producing forty Lysander army co-operation aircraft a month. After some debate the Army won its case and the Air Ministry decided in October 1939 to cancel all orders for the Whirlwind and instructed Westland to concentrate solely on Lysander production. Inevitably Westland protested strongly at this cancellation, as a substantial number of major components for around one hundred Whirlwind aircraft had already been paid for and manufactured. In the light of this, and the fact that many of the major castings and forgings for a substantial number of Rolls Royce Peregrine engines had also already been made, the Air Council Committee on Supply decided in late November to reinstate one hundred and fourteen Whirlwinds simply to use up the material and avoid waste. No further Whirlwinds were to be built. Ironically, during the BEF's retreat in France the Lysander's vulnerability as an army co-operation aircraft was exposed and the need for the Lysander in large numbers evaporated after the evacuation of the British Expeditionary Force (BEF) from Dunkirk in June 1940, just as the Whirlwind was entering service. However, by then it was too late to resurrect Whirlwind production.

Incarcerated as he was within the Chief of the Air Staff's (CAS) outer office in the Air Ministry, my father would doubtless not only have taken a great interest in this new design of fighter, especially as he was an aircraft armament specialist, but would also have been aware of the decisions to cancel then re-instate Whirlwind production. He remained working for CAS for the first nine months of the war but was probably eager to escape back to frontline flying again. Time was not on his side. Air Chief Marshal Sir Hugh Dowding, the Commander in Chief of Fighter Command, only wanted young men as his squadron commanders and my father turned thirty on 12th May 1940.

In those days thirty was considered by many to be old. He had little experience of flying the new types of fighter aircraft, with their retractable landing gear, variable pitch airscrews, powerful engines and enclosed cockpits and could well have been considered too old to embrace this new technology. Nevertheless, in the desperate days following the evacuation of the BEF from France, an opportunity came along. During the ill-fated campaign in Norway 263 Squadron, equipped with Gladiator biplane fighters, had fought hard but lost many of its pilots, including its commanding officer, and all its aircraft. On its return from Norway it was reformed at Grangemouth, a grass airfield between Stirling and Edinburgh on the south bank of the Firth of Forth, now the site of a huge oil refinery. It was initially equipped with Hurricanes and was slowly returning to an operational status, with a role to defend the important naval anchorages and shipyards at Rosyth on the Firth of Forth and Glasgow on the Clyde, which were now in reach of Luftwaffe bombers based in Norway and Denmark. A decision was taken to re-equip 263 Squadron with the Whirlwind; my father was appointed as the new squadron commander and was tasked with bringing the Whirlwind into operational service.

After a hectic and very short refresher flying course at the end of June 1940, consisting of three flights in a Harvard trainer, one of which is annotated as 'target aircraft', he flew seven Hurricane sorties then flew up to Grangemouth in a Miles Master trainer to visit his new command. He returned to Martlesham Heath, the RAF's experimental and test airfield, where he sampled the Whirlwind for the first time. The logbook entry I have chosen was his fourth flight in P6966, the first production Whirlwind (plate 19). He had set off for Grangemouth the previous day but diverted into Dishforth, a bomber base near Boroughbridge in North Yorkshire, because of bad weather and thunderstorms. The Whirlwind was still classified as 'top-secret' at this time so it would have been interesting to see the reaction of those at Dishforth to the unexpected arrival of this virtually unknown top-secret fighter. Next day the weather cleared so he continued north, stopping for a short while at Drem, the main fighter base to the east of Edinburgh, before continuing on to Grangemouth and 263 Squadron. He was faced with a difficult challenge at Grangemouth. The squadron was declared operational with a flight of Hurricanes; the small numbers of Whirlwinds available were strictly non-operational whilst all the teething troubles associated with such a new aircraft were sorted out. There were many problems to address. The tail wheel leg was prone to break on the rough grass surface of the airfield, the engines were found to lose power above 25,000ft and there were problems with the guns jamming when fired. It was not long before the first production aircraft, P6966, was lost.

The aircraft suffered a burst tyre on take off and the landing gear jammed half way up. It was considered too dangerous to attempt a landing in this condition so the pilot was given the option of abandoning the aircraft, which crashed in farmland near Stirling. The pilot was promptly arrested by the Home Guard and only released from captivity as a consequence of my father's intervention. Much of the wreckage remained buried until the 1970s when it was excavated. Interestingly, one tyre was subsequently found to be a Hurricane tyre, which could have been the reason it burst. Quite possibly it had been fitted incorrectly, since the squadron was flying both types of aircraft. The surface condition of the airfield at Grangemouth was considered to be very poor and unsuitable for the Whirlwind. My father flew both the Hurricane and Whirlwind over this period, not always successfully, as he evidently crashed a Hurricane whilst landing at night on 27th August, night flying aids not having changed much since his days at Northolt eight years previously.

The Battle of Britain was now raging down in the south and of course 263 Squadron was keen to get involved. However, the Whirlwind was still very new, untried in combat and only available in very small numbers, the Fighter Command aircraft availability document of 1 September 1940 showing only six being on strength. Lord Beaverbrook, Minister for Aircraft Production, had written to Dowding in June asking for an assessment of the Whirlwind, noting that it was soon to cease being built. Dowding responded that he considered it to be the only aircraft in Fighter Command that had a potential capability successfully to attack armoured vehicles with its 20mm cannon. As a consequence he would only sanction a move south by 263 squadron in the event of the much expected invasion occurring. The squadron moved from Grangemouth to Drem, a far better airfield, in September, with a steady build up in the number of Whirlwinds now taking place. There are some interesting photographs of Whirlwinds parked inside revetments made of logs and surrounded by trees at Drem. The squadron (plate 20) had also built similar revetments Norway, where there was a plentiful supply of timber. Apparently this was just a publicity exercise as the revetments were too far away from the squadron operations room to be of any use should a short notice call to scramble take place.

In addition to the stress of bringing this brand new fighter into service, my father married Janet Norton on 22nd October, whom he had first met in 1933 in Egypt. It is fascinating to see the photograph of those attending the ceremony (plate 21), which was held at the South Queensferry registry office, given the difficulties of long distance travel in wartime. The serious looking group includes my father's mother, his mother-in-law, his brother and sister and their respective spouses and his wife's younger brother, a naval officer conveniently locally based at Port Edgar. All others had travelled from well down in the south of England. The wedding reception was held at The Hawes Inn, South Queensferry. I still have in my possession a silver cigarette box, inscribed 'To Squadron Leader H. Eeles, from the Officers, N.C.O's & Airmen of 263 Squadron, on his marriage October 1940.' The newly-weds set up home in a house in Gullane, the closest village to RAF Drem, there being no service accommodation for families on the base. The house, 'The Fairway', must have had connections with Muirfield, the famous local golf course. They did not live there for long.

By the end of November 263 Squadron was finally declared fully operational with the Whirlwind. It got rid of its Hurricanes and moved south on 28th November to Exeter, another grass airfield. Sadly, there is little detail of what my father achieved at Exeter, other than an enigmatic logbook entry that simply states 'Total Whirlwind flying for month at Exeter 12 hrs.' I believe he did fly on some operational patrols, including the squadron's first operational patrol with the Whirlwind, but there is no written detail. The Battle of Britain had by now been won, but in 1960 263 Squadron was added to the list of squadrons that participated in the Battle. My father was advised that he might be eligible for the Battle of Britain clasp but he never claimed it. He felt that the squadron was too far away from the fighting to justify a claim, despite some Hurricane operational sorties being flown by the squadron from Grangemouth and Drem. Nevertheless, it is with great pride that I see his name on the Battle of Britain Memorial on the Embankment and on the Wall of Honour at the Battle of Britain Memorial at Capel le Fern, on the cliff top near Dover. Having brought the Whirlwind into service my father was rewarded with promotion to Wing Commander and immediately sent back north to command RAF Drem, the Station he had just left. The Squadron gave him a plated silver salver when he left, with a head-on view of a Whirlwind engraved on the underneath, as the Whirlwind was still on the secret list. He never had the chance to fly on operations again during the war, all his appointments being either command of fighter bases or staff duties with the Second Tactical Air Force and Fighter Command.

By early 1941 the main German bomber activity was at night. The Whirlwind was not a suitable night fighter, being single seat; early air intercept radar sets fitted to the Beaufighter needed a separate operator in addition to the pilot. The Whirlwind thus never found itself used in its originally intended role as a bomber destroyer. By the spring of 1941 Fighter Command had now taken the offensive with sweeps over occupied France and the Whirlwind was found to be a very good ground attack fighter when used in this role. It had a heavy armament, a very good turn of speed at low level and the bonus of twin-engine safety in the event of suffering battle damage over enemy held territory. It was not long before it was adapted to carry two bombs on wing pylons, which could be delivered in a dive attack. The one hundred and fourteen Whirlwinds produced equipped only two squadrons, 263 and 137, but they remained in service until the end of 1943, a very good record for such a small number of aircraft given the rate of attrition experienced in wartime from combat losses and other accidents. It was very popular with its pilots and was in many ways well ahead of its time. The concept of the twin engine, single seat fighter of which it was a pioneer has proved to be very successful, some typical examples from the 1940s being the De Havilland Hornet and Gloster Meteor.

More recently the English Electric Lightning, BAe Jaguar and Eurofighter Typhoon have used the same concept. One Whirlwind survived intact at the end of World War 2; Westlands acquired it, placed it on the civil register as G-AGOI and used it as a Company 'hack' until 1948, when sadly it was broken up at Yeovil. Another was sent to the USA by sea in 1942 apparently for its armament to be assessed by the USAAF and the US Navy; little is known about what it did but it last flew in early 1944. Peter Twiss, a naval test pilot, ferried it from Cherry Point to Eglin Field in January, some months after the Whirlwind had been withdrawn from RAF service. Peter Twiss had a long career as a test pilot and was the first pilot to achieve a world airspeed record of more than 1000 mph. The Whirlwind's ultimate fate is unknown but there is a rumour that its Peregrine engines were used to power the Base Commander's speedboat. Thus the only remains of a Whirlwind existing now are the pieces of wreckage of P6966 that in the 1970s were excavated by a team of enthusiasts from the field in Stirlingshire where it fell in August 1940. One of the Peregrine engines is displayed in the Rolls Royce museum in Derby. However, an organization called the Whirlwind Fighter Project Team has started to construct a full size, non-flying, metal replica. This is a long-term, costly project but hopefully one day a Whirlwind will be seen again.

CHAPTER 10

THE COLD WAR, DEFENDING GIBRALTAR

LOGBOOK ENTRY, TOM EELES

10 February 1976,
Hunter FGA9 XG155,
Self
Anchorage recce and photo task.
1 hour, 10 minutes

I do not have a direct equivalent logbook entry to my father's in Chapter 9. Nevertheless, in 1976 I found myself a member of 79 Squadron, one of the three reserve squadrons based at RAF Brawdy. Brawdy was located at the extreme south-western end of Wales and was the home base of the RAF's Tactical Weapons Unit. We were equipped with the Hawker Hunter F6, T7 and FGA9. As there was just the faintest possibility of flying in what might possibly turn out to be a hostile environment, and as the Hunter was a single seat fighter armed with four cannon (like the Whirlwind), this seemed to be the best equivalent I could find.

The Hawker Hunter was a classic single seat fighter, designed by Sir Sidney Camm of the Hawker Aircraft Company. Sidney Camm had designed a whole series of elegant biplanes in the 1930s (see Chapter 7), also the Hurricane, Typhoon and Tempest fighters of World War Two, the Fury and Sea Fury and his first jet fighter, the Sea Hawk. The Hunter was his first successful swept wing design and its maiden flight took place on 20th July 1951, piloted by the famous test pilot Neville Duke. On landing Duke reported that he was delighted with the new aircraft and remarked that it handled beautifully. This came as no surprise to Sidney Camm, who once said 'I'm only interested in designing fighters; there's no finesse, no skill in designing anything else.' The Hunter entered RAF service as an interceptor fighter in the early 1950s, however, the aircraft was bedeviled with problems in its early service career despite its beautiful lines. If it fired its guns at altitude engine the engine would flame out, it suffered from short endurance due to lack of fuel and it had a tendency to pitch up in tight turns, a very undesirable characteristic for a fighter aircraft. All this contributed to a poor initial reputation, especially compared to the American F86 Sabre fighter, used in some numbers by the RAF. It was described by one of Hawker's designers as 'A beautiful load of trouble'. This was not a good time for British designed fighter aircraft; the Hunter's rival, the Supermarine Swift, built by the same company that produced the superb Spitfire, was so bad that it never entered service as an interceptor fighter.

Eventually the later versions of the Hunter, the F6, T7 and FGA9 had the early problems sorted out and the Hunter became a much loved fighter aircraft with delightful handling qualities. Large numbers were exported to foreign air forces with many being built under licence in India, Belgium and Sweden. Replaced as a front line interceptor fighter in the RAF by the Lightning and as a ground attack and reconnaissance fighter by the Harrier and Jaguar, by the mid 1970s it was used in RAF service solely as a fighter lead-in trainer on the Tactical Weapons Unit. The Tactical Weapons Unit, based at RAF Brawdy, provided courses for pilots graduating from flying training before they moved on to fly their more complex operational aircraft, and refresher courses for pilots returning to operational flying after escaping from ground duties. Despite this second line training role the Hunter still could provide a significant operational punch with its heavy armament of four 30mm Aden cannons, 68mm SNEB rockets and a photo-reconnaissance capability with its Vinten F95 camera. Thus the Tactical Weapons Unit had a war role to provide Hunters for daytime short range air defence duties at the RAF's main fighter airfields in the UK and also overseas at Gibraltar.

The Phoenicians and the Romans first settled the Rock of Gibraltar in classical times. It was named after Tariq ibn Ziyad, the Moorish general who led the Islamic invasion of what is now Spain in 711 AD. The name is a corruption of Jabal Tariq, Tariq's mountain. In 1462 it was captured by Spanish forces but was ceded to Great Britain by Spain in 1713 by the Treaty of Utrecht at the end of the War of the Spanish Succession. It has remained British dependant territory ever since, despite many attempts by Spain to recover it. Dominating the entrance to the Mediterranean from the Atlantic, it is a key strategic asset and has played an important role in many conflicts, the most recent being the Falklands War in 1982, when many of the Royal Navy's warships mustered there before sailing south. The long association with Great Britain and the Royal Navy is poignantly emphasized by the graveyard in Gibraltar where many of those killed in the Battle of Trafalgar are buried. In the 1960s Spain stepped up its demands for the 'decolonisation' of Gibraltar; Britain responded in 1967 by giving the inhabitants a vote on whether to remain British or be ceded to Spain. The pro British won the vote by a margin of 12,138 to 44. Spain's response was to seal the land border, depriving Gibraltar of Spanish trade and workers. Despite the economic hardship and inconvenience caused to the locals, their loyalty to Great Britain remained steadfast.

In the 1970s there was always an implied threat from Spain to British civil and military aircraft approaching or leaving Gibraltar, so a small detachment of three Hunter FGA9 fighter aircraft (plate 22) were based at the airfield as a deterrent to any Spanish attempt at interference of inbound or outbound civil and military flights. The airfield at Gibraltar (plate 23) was located on reclaimed land between the Spanish border and close to the sheer north face of the Rock, which rose to over 1000ft. The runway was built in the Second World War and subsequently extended out into the sea to the west into Algeciras Bay. It was 6000ft long but without any arrestor barriers to prevent aircraft running off the end into the sea. It was crossed by the main road from the border to the town and was often greatly affected by very severe cross winds and turbulence generated by the Rock. The nearest diversion airfields were Tangier across the Straits of Gibraltar in Morocco and Faro in Portugal. Spanish airfields were clearly not available and Spanish surface to air missile batteries on the mainland hills overlooked the runway, thus it was a challenging location from which to operate a single seat fighter aircraft with not a great amount of fuel and minimal navigation aids. There were always three pilots from Brawdy at Gibraltar and each spent three weeks there on detached duty. Flying could only take place if there was an expected inbound or outbound aircraft or if the locally based Viscount airliner was flying between Gibraltar and Tangier. A maximum of two Hunters could get airborne at a time, as the third pilot was required to act as a flying supervisor in the ATC tower.

We were left very much to our own devices once in the air; we did air combat, we provided targets for any RN ships that were exercising in the local area and we regularly visited the Soviet navy's anchorage at Alboran to photograph any warships. The sortie recorded at the head of this chapter is typical of a Gibraltar sortie. Flown as a pair, a low level transit out to the Soviet Navy's anchorage to photograph and record any warships there, then a return to Gibraltar for a few visual circuits to keep the air traffic controllers entertained. I also recall being a 'bounce' aircraft for a Buccaneer formation; the Hunter had no radio altimeter so we flew as low as we dared over the sea. Some pilots were tempted to climb to high altitude and do a supersonic run, aiming the resulting sonic bang at Algeciras across the bay from Gibraltar; if the bang was heard in Gibraltar there would inevitably be a one-sided interview with the Air Commander, usually a man from a maritime patrol background with little time for fighter pilot japes. The greatest challenge to us was boredom. Compared to the varied activity at home in Wales the flying at Gibraltar was monotonous. We could only fly over the sea, Spain being clearly off limits, as also were Portugal and Tunisia unless we were diverting to their airfields. The weather was often unsuitable for flying and the runway at Gibraltar was plagued by cross winds and turbulence from the Rock. After three weeks of relative inactivity one was glad to get back on the charter flight home to the UK and to a more vibrant, albeit cooler and wetter time back at Brawdy.

After duty the social scene in Gibraltar was somewhat limited. Female company consisted of some of the Air Traffic Controllers and the local British school teachers, all of whom spent considerably longer than our three weeks in the confines of Gibraltar. They therefore enjoyed a regularly changing variety of male company, the disadvantage being that most of these had wives and families back in Pembrokeshire. The various goings-on and many misdemeanors were duly recorded in the Hunter detachment's Gibraltar Diaries, which all those who had been to Gibraltar agreed should never be allowed to leave the Rock. When the Hunter detachment finally stood down these potentially incriminating volumes were destroyed.

By the late 1970s Spain had shaken off the worst excesses of the Franco regime. Relations with Gibraltar and the UK improved to the extent that the land border between Gibraltar and Spain was reopened in 1985, much to the Gibraltarians' delight. The need to maintain an air defence presence in Gibraltar evaporated and back in the UK the Hunter was being phased out as a tactics and weapons trainer in favour of the BAe Hawk T1. The detachment was stood down and the Hunters returned to the UK, almost certainly to be scrapped. A few two seat Hunters continued in RAF service until 1994 in support of the Buccaneer squadrons at Lossiemouth, acting as surrogate trainers for the Buccaneer, which never had a dual control version. The Swiss, Chilean and Indian

Air Forces continued to operate upgraded single seat Hunters throughout the 1990s, but eventually more modern fighters replaced these veterans. The RAF still maintains a small presence in Gibraltar and a variety of its aircraft occasionally visit but none are based there permanently. The Royal Navy continues to use the dockyard facilities and Gibraltar has enjoyed something of an economic recovery. Nevertheless, the Spanish government still yearns to recover Gibraltar despite the often stated wishes of its inhabitants; a number of incidents involving small vessels challenging the territorial water limits take place regularly and there still remains the very remote prospect of a possible Spanish take over by force which might now be rather difficult to challenge.

CHAPTER ELEVEN

A CANADIAN REFRESHER ?

LOGBOOK ENTRY, HARRY EELES

26 May 1947
Beechcraft C45 1387
Flt Lt Watson/Self
Local, Rockcliffe
2 hrs

By May 1947 Harry Eeles had been working in the USA for nearly 18 months as Staff Officer to Air Marshal Sir Guy Garrod, who was the Chief of the Air Force Section, UK Delegation to the Military Staffs Committee of the United Nations. In the optimistic days after the founding of the United Nations it was hoped that the most prominent nations would contribute armed forces to a United Nations military organization, hence the establishment of the Military Staffs Committee. Both officers had experienced a shaky start to this new venture when, in the spring of 1946, they were involved as passengers in a serious car accident. This left my father glad in a plaster cast from head to waist to stabilize a broken back, in the sweltering heat of the summer in a US Navy hospital.

The rest of us, my mother, myself and my brother and sister were still left behind in England, there being no chance of a passage across the Atlantic whilst thousands of American and Canadian troops were repatriated and demobbed after the end of the Second World War. Eventually, in December 1946, we were able to take a passage in the SS Samaria from Liverpool to Halifax, Nova Scotia, then a train journey south to Long Island, New York, where my father had found rented accommodation for us. My memories of these days are very scant but I do recall a military band welcoming us to Halifax as there were still many Canadian troops aboard. I have vague recollections of going to nursery school and swearing allegiance to the President of the USA, of going to New York and going up the Empire State Building, where the UN Military Staffs worked (the UN building not yet been built), and of eventually going back to England on the Cunard liner RMS Queen Elizabeth.

Unsurprisingly there are very few entries for this period in Harry Eeles's logbook. He did not fly for nearly a year, from November 1945 until the end of October 1946. Then some ten flights in a Beechcraft are recorded, all with an officer with an RAF rank. Only towards the end of the sequence does a clue appear as to where this flying took place, with an entry Ottawa to London lasting 2 hours and 30 minutes. Clearly this was not a transatlantic flight so evidently just a local one somewhere in Canada. Turning the page, there are another ten flights recorded over a six day period in May 1947 (plate 24), this time the aircraft is identified as a Beechcraft C45 (plate 25), again with RAF ranked co-pilots. The airfield of origin is identified as Rockcliffe and the flights are all in the region of Toronto, Montreal and Rockcliffe. From these entries I conclude that Harry Eeles succeeded in arranging some form of refresher flying with the Royal Canadian Air Force (RCAF) during his time in the USA with the UN.

Rockcliffe was established as an airfield in 1920 when it was opened as the Ottawa Air Station. It was one of the earliest airfields opened in Canada and being very close to the river could accommodate both land and floatplanes. It was used extensively during the Second World War by the Commonwealth Air Training Programme and also for test flying and transport operations. Hard runways were added and although the first jet flights in Canada in 1946 took place here the runways proved to be too short for regular jet operations and the airfield slowly declined in importance. By

1964 military flying had ceased and today only the Rockcliffe Flying Club remains as a flying organization. The old airfield is now the home of the Canada Aviation Museum, which has a very extensive collection of a wide variety of aircraft associated with Canadian military and civil aviation. Doubtless in 1946 and '47, it would still have been a busy military airfield when Harry Eeles flew the Beechcraft C45 there for the first time.

The Beechcraft C45 was the military version of the highly successful Beechcraft Model 18 that first flew in 1937. It was a twin engined light passenger aircraft with retractable landing gear and seated up to 11 passengers. It remained in production from 1937 to 1969, a world record at the time. Over 9000 were built and over 4500 were used in military service by a large number of air forces, including the USAAF, USN, RAF and RCAF. The RCAF alone possessed some 394 C45s and kept them in service from 1941 to 1972. Its maximum speed was 195 knots and it was powered by two Pratt and Whitney Wasp Junior radial engines rated at 450 HP. At the time of writing (August 2017) there were still 240 Beechcraft Model 18s active in the USA alone. Clearly it was a very successful design and in 1946 it gave Harry Eeles his first experience of flying an American aircraft in the very different environment of the American continent when compared to flying in wartime England. At least he had already gained some twin engine flying experience in the RAF on the Anson, Oxford, Domine and of course the Whirlwind fighter, as described in Chapter 9.

The logbook entry, chosen at random, is the first flight Harry Eeles undertook since his previous flying at Rockcliffe some 7 months previously. It is broadly similar to the others in this group and would probably consisted of some general handling to brush off any cobwebs before embarking on a more meaningful exercise such as instrument flying or a cross country navigation exercise. It must have been a welcome relief to get away from the noise and heat of downtown New York, to say nothing of a house full of very young children, to get back in the air again. The week of flying the C45 at Rockcliffe at the end of May 1947 was the last time Harry Eeles flew until August 1948, when he assumed command of the Fighter Command Sector Station of RAF Thorney Island, as described in Chapter 13.

CHAPTER TWELVE

TRANSPORTING THE 'SPOOKS'

LOGBOOK ENTRY, TOM EELES

21 February 1991
Jetstream T1
Flt Lt Izzat/Self
Operation Aster, Wyton – Ramstein – Marham
3hrs, 40 min.

After some six years continuous flying as a wing commander I found myself promoted out of the cockpit and into an office at the Headquarters of RAF Support Command as Group Captain (Flying Training). Using the excuse of needing to get out and about into the various flying training stations, I managed to keep flying in a number of training aircraft, including the Jetstream, which I had been current on in my previous appointment. In the wider world outside a number of potentially dangerous events were beginning to unfold in the Middle East, in particular in Iraq, where Sadaam Hussein was becoming increasingly belligerent. Eventually, in August 1990, his forces invaded Kuwait and occupied it, threatening further military incursions into neighbouring Saudi Arabia.

The RAF's front line became heavily involved in the Coalition's response to this aggression, however, at first it had little effect on the more peaceful and orderly lifestyle of the RAF's flying training organization. This began to change around November 1990, when a task associated with what eventually became known as Gulf War 1 soon appeared. This was known as Operation Aster. It involved transporting two individuals from the

Joint Air Reconnaissance and Intelligence Centre (JARIC), which was located at the same site, RAF Brampton, as HQ RAFSC, from RAF Wyton (our nearest airfield) to the large USAF base at Ramstein in West Germany. On arrival there these two individuals would disappear, sometimes for a short time, sometimes for hours, then re-appear clutching a large sack each. Doubtless these sacks had something very important, and secret, within them. The Jetstream would then fly back to Wyton and the two individuals would disappear quickly by car back to JARIC. As this placed an extra, unexpected, burden on the Jetstream squadron's aircrew, I offered to help out as a co-pilot whenever needed. Not only did this activity give me the opportunity to get out of the office for an unpredictable length of time, but it also gave me the chance to contribute to the war effort, however minimal that contribution might be. In December another task related to the expected outbreak of the land campaign to recover Kuwait was devolved to Support Command. I was tasked with devising what would have been an airborne taxi service to transport doctors and medical staffs around the country to meet incoming transport aircraft with casualties from the land campaign. I decided to use the Jetstreams from RAF Finningley for this task, basing them and their crews at RAF Wyton, where they would be close to our Headquarters, which would manage and direct this task. In the event the land campaign never produced the forecast casualties so the plan was never activated.

The Jetstream (plate 26) was designed and built by Handley Page, a company that could claim always to have had one of its aircraft in RAF service from the day the RAF was formed on 1 April 1918. Powered by two Astazou turbo prop engines of French origin and capable of accommodating twelve passengers in its pressurized cabin, it was aimed at the commuter aircraft market. It first flew in 1967 and its future initially seemed to be very bright, especially in the USA, where there was estimated to be a large market for this type of mini airliner. A potential order from the

USAF was also anticipated. Unfortunately Handley Page was suffering severe financial difficulties as the company had refused to join one of the large merged groups of aircraft manufacturers that the government had directed to be established in an attempt to rationalize the aircraft industry. As a consequence it was starved of any further military contracts. Development of the Jetstream was slow, the USAF contract was cancelled and eventually Handley Page went bankrupt and was shut down. Scottish Aviation eventually took on Jetstream development and production and ultimately a total of 386 aircraft were built and sold. The majority of these were the Jetstream 31 version, which had the awkward Astazou engines replaced by more powerful and reliable Garret TPE331 turbo props. In the early 1970s the RAF was looking for a replacement for the Vickers Varsity multi-engine trainer and selected the Astazou powered Jetstream.

Initial experience with the Jetstream as a multi-engine trainer was not at all satisfactory and for a while, after cut backs to the transport fleet in 1975, the Jetstreams were all stored at RAF St Athan. The need to restart multi-engine training soon returned and the fleet was reactivated at RAF Finningley, whilst some aircraft were transferred to the Royal Navy for observer training. By the 1980s the early troubles with the aircraft had largely been sorted out and it had settled down to provide reliable service as a multi-engine trainer despite some of its handling characteristics being less than ideal. Nevertheless, it was a good light transport aircraft, cruising at a moderately high speed and at a reasonable altitude. Unfortunately the Astazou turbo props, rotating at a constant speed of 43,000 RPM, made it very noisy inside and by 1990 the military standard sound-proofing and interior trimming were showing distinct signs of wear and tear due to the tramping in and out of countless student pilots. There was much evidence of black 'bodge' tape holding things together. This was the noisy, rather shabby interior that the 'spooks' from JARIC had to sit in on the way to and back from Ramstein. At least they had large cabin windows to look out from.

The flight on 21 February turned out to be the last Operation Aster flight that I undertook (plate 27). We left Wyton in mid-afternoon in fine weather but the forecast for the evening and night was not encouraging, with wide spread low cloud and fog expected across East Anglia. We had no idea how long we would be sitting on the ground at Ramstein waiting for our 'spook' passengers to return; we hoped it would not be too long. The outbound flight was uneventful and we prepared the aircraft for its return flight, then waited in the USAF Transient Aircraft facility, a rather austere room with few creature comforts. This time it was a long wait, more than two hours, before our charges returned clutching their precious bags. It was now fully dark and as we droned across Germany and Belgium the weather reports from East Anglia confirmed our worst fears. Visibility and cloud bases were rapidly reducing. We consulted with our passengers and advised that diversion was getting increasingly likely, and possibly to a civil airfield as there would be very few RAF airfields open given the weather conditions.

They were most concerned at the possibility of arriving at a civil airfield and urged that we find somewhere military, preferably as close to JARIC as possible. An attempt was made to recover into Wyton but it was no good; at 200ft on our instrument approach nothing could be seen. Fuel was now getting a bit short. Then an unexpected piece of good news came in. RAF Marham, just up the road, was open as it was generating Tornados for transit out to the Middle East, and the weather there was just within limits. We set off and recovered there without any problems and were welcomed into the Operations Centre, where the Station Commander, Group Captain Jock Stirrup, whom I knew of old, offered us the use of a car to take us the 40 odd miles back to Brampton. Graham Izzatt and I accepted his offer with alacrity, as it had been a very long day for us both. The 'spooks', however, declined and decided to wait until their JARIC car had set off from Wyton and arrived at Marham to take them back to their home base. Goodness knows what time they got there, I left Graham Izzatt at the Wyton Officers' Mess and drove home, arriving at around two in the morning. I was eternally grateful to the Station Commander, who ultimately became a Marshal of the Royal Air Force and a Lord.

I only flew a Jetstream once more, in August 1990, from Finningley to Lossiemouth and back, to attend a funeral. The Jetstream soldiered on as a multi-engine trainer until 2004, when it was taken out of service and replaced by a contractor provided fleet of Beech King Airs. This marked the end of Handley Page's aircraft's unbroken record of RAF service of 86 years, a remarkable achievement.

CHAPTER THIRTEEN

DISPLAY FLYING, 1949

LOGBOOK ENTRY, HARRY EELES

17 September 1949
Vampire
Self
Battle of Britain Race
25 minutes

Shortly after the end of the Second World War Harry Eeles, who was based at Bentley Priory, the Headquarters of Fighter Command, flew a short sortie in a Gloster Meteor III, the first practical jet fighter produced in the UK. This was his introduction to the new sensation of jet powered flight and must have been an amazing experience for someone who had started flying a mere sixteen years earlier in a biplane dating from the earliest days of military aviation in the First World War. He was then appointed as Staff Officer to Air Chief Marshal Sir Guy Garrod, the Chief of the Air Force Section of the UK Delegation to the Military Staff Committee, United Nations. After two years in the USA he was appointed in 1948 as Station Commander at RAF Thorney Island, a Fighter Command sector station with two resident squadrons of Meteor IV fighters.

At this time Britain was still a world leader in jet aircraft design and technology, although the USA was soon to become predominant in this field. The Soviet Union was somewhat behind in jet engine technology, but soon caught up after a visit to British jet engine manufacturers by Russian aircraft and engine designers, which resulted in the sale of the latest British jet engines to the Soviets. The Meteor had served for a short time on operations during the last months of the Second World War in its Mk III version, the next version, the Mk IV, being the first really successful model. Although somewhat less sophisticated than its wartime German equivalent, the Me 262, it was robust and simple, its Derwent gas turbines were more reliable and easier to handle than contemporary axial flow gas turbines and many Meteors were exported to foreign customers. Large numbers were built, including two-seat night fighter, photo-reconnaisance and advanced trainer versions. Two are still used as ejection seat test aircraft by the Martin Baker Aircraft Company, an astonishing record of longevity for an aircraft designed and flown for the first time in the early 1940s. Jet powered aircraft proved to be very different from their piston engined predecessors. There was no torque reaction to changes in power settings but engine response to throttle movement was much slower than with a piston engine and fuel consumption was much higher.

Jet aircraft could achieve much greater speeds and altitudes and the view from an aircraft with the cockpit well forward, combined with a nose wheel, made take off and landing far easier than in a piston engined aircraft with a tail wheel. Escape in the event of emergency was much more problematic at the high speeds that jet aircraft routinely encountered, a manual bale-out being virtually impossible. The Meteor, with its twin-engine configuration, could be a challenging aircraft to fly on one engine. Practice single engine flying, with one engine shut down, claimed more lives lost than any genuine engine failures. The Meteor also suffered from a phenomenon known as the 'Phantom Dive', which also claimed many lives. If the airbrakes were left out when the landing gear was selected down, the aircraft would roll rapidly out of control into a steep dive, as the main wheels extended one at a time, causing a roll towards the extended main wheel leg. Since this was likely to occur at low level when the aircraft joined in the landing pattern, the result was normally a fatal crash.

RAF Thorney Island was an idyllic place. Located in west Sussex on a peninsula in Chichester Harbour, it was selected as a suitable site for development as an airfield in the late 1930s. A Hawker Fury had crashed there and the accident investigators were impressed by the suitability of the area for an airfield. A typical airfield of the 1930s era of expansion, it was used throughout the Second World War by Coastal Command, suffering damage from Luftwaffe bombing which was still very much in evidence in 1948. One of the hangars was still roofless and without window glass and there were many water-filled bomb craters still in existence. Before the arrival of the RAF there was a small hamlet with an ancient church at the eastern end of the peninsula, the church now being used by the RAF personnel. Also on the eastern side was Thorney creek, a muddy tidal inlet, home to a sailing club and a number of pleasure craft. A public road ran across the airfield to the church and creek. After the war the station was transferred to Fighter Command.

It would appear that my father was not particularly keen on flying the Meteor, perhaps due to its dubious safety reputation. His logbook reveals only five sorties in Meteors over the period when he was Station Commander from August 1948 to June 1950. I recall that he found the Meteor uncomfortable, possibly as a consequence of injury to his back suffered in a car accident whilst serving in the USA. On the other hand there are a great many sorties recorded in the Vampire (plate 28), de Havilland's elegant little single engine twin boom fighter, a direct contemporary and rival of the Meteor. There were no Vampire squadrons based at Thorney Island so there must have been a Vampire on the Station Flight, which probably became the Station Commander's personal aircraft. The Vampire was also built in large numbers, both for the RAF and foreign air forces. It was developed into a two seat night fighter and an advanced trainer. It was a popular aircraft with good handling qualities and it did not suffer from some of the problems that beset the Meteor.

Turning now to the logbook entry, in the 1940s every RAF flying station held an 'At Home Day' on the weekend closest to Battle of Britain Day, 15th September, as the memory of the Battle of Britain was still very fresh in many people's minds (plate 29). The flying display would doubtless consist of solo and formation aerobatics by the resident squadrons, displays and flypasts by aircraft from other stations both near and far, joy rides in civilian aircraft and all manner of ground displays demonstrating the work of the station. RAF Thorney Island clearly organized an air race in 1949, my father competing in his favourite aircraft, the Vampire. The race lasted some twenty-five minutes, by which time the Vampire's meagre fuel capacity must have been virtually exhausted, given that the entire twenty-five minutes would have been spent at full power at low level, conditions for the highest fuel consumption in a jet fighter. The other race participants and the ultimate winner remain unknown.

By 1948 the threat of confrontation in Europe had returned barely three years after the cessation of hostilities. This time the threat was from the Soviet Union. An Iron Curtain had descended across Europe and a period known as the Cold War had started, with every possibility that it might turn hot. Fighter Command was in the process of recovering from its run down after the end of the Second World War and its day fighter squadrons were now nearly all equipped with jet fighters. After the relative calm and sophistication of two years in the USA it must have been quite a shock to return to a United Kingdom still experiencing rationing and threatened again by possible war. It would have been an exciting time to be Station Commander of a fighter station. The first major confrontation of the Cold War had started, with the 1948 Berlin Airlift demonstrating the recently formed NATO alliance resolve to face down threats from the Soviet Union. After a period in the doldrums after the end of the war, the RAF was expanding again. The British aircraft industry was embarking on some exotic new projects, both military and civil.

Whilst being taken to RAF West Raynham in Norfolk by its Station Commander, Group Captain Humphrey Edwards-Jones (a close family friend) for a summer holiday, I recall stopping off at some airfield on the way. We watched a large, beautiful silver aircraft land and taxi in. I had no idea what it was at the time; however, I learnt later that we had witnessed the completion of the de Havilland Comet prototype's first flight. 'EJ' as he was known, was a great family friend and we often visited him in Norfolk where he was Station Commander at RAF West Raynham. Before the war, he had been a test pilot based at Martlesham Heath, the RAF's test establishment. The prototype Spitfire had just arrived there and there were considerable worries that it would prove to be too advanced for the average RAF pilot to fly. EJ was briefed to take it up and report back as to whether considered it suitable for the average RAF pilot to fly, given its sophisticated design compared to current service aircraft. Luckily he landed safely and reported there was no problem. The consequences of an unfavourable report might have been very different.

Unusually, those two years at Thorney Island were my father's fifth stint as a Station Commander. During the war he commanded Drem, Ayr, Catterick as a Wing Commander and Colerne as an acting Group Captain, all fighter bases, never staying in post for more than a few months, which was a typical experience for that time. Thus staying at Thorney Island for nearly two years gave the family a degree of unexpected stability. It was without doubt that living at Thorney Island, cheek by jowl with the constant comings and goings of the Meteors, that inspired me to become an RAF pilot. My first ever flight, a short 'joy ride' in a Dragon Rapide on that Battle of Britain 'At Home Day' costing ten shillings (50p) simply confirmed my ambition. In June 1950 my father moved on, first to the School of Land Air Warfare at RAF

Old Sarum and then barely six months later to SHAPE Headquarters in France. Then in September 1952, on promotion to acting Air Commodore, he was posted to a much more prestigious appointment as Commandant and Air Officer Commanding the RAF College Cranwell.

CHAPTER FOURTEEN

DISPLAY FLYING FORTY YEARS LATER

LOGBOOK ENTRY, TOM EELES

29 June 1989,
Hawk T1 XX260,
Self /Flt Lt Newton, Red 9
Red Arrows display at Marham and CFS check
50 minutes

During the 1950s the Cold War intensified and the Korean War broke out in the Far East; the RAF began to expand again, particularly Fighter Command and Flying Training Command. Battle of Britain Days at RAF Stations provided opportunities for the Service to show off its new aircraft and the skill of its pilots. Meanwhile the British aircraft industry was experiencing something of a golden era, with many companies producing a wide range of aircraft, some successful, some less so. Despite the terrible accident at the Society of British Aircraft Constructors' Farnborough Air Show in 1952, when a DH110 broke up and fell into the crowd, air displays continued to be hugely popular with the public. No self respecting fighter squadron or flying training school would be without its aerobatic display team, often sporting exotic titles such as the Firebirds, the Blue Diamonds, the Macaws, the Poachers, the Yellow Jacks, the Gemini Pair and the Red Pelicans, to name but a few.

The most famous and well-remembered team was the Black Arrows of 111 Squadron who still hold a record of looping 22 Hunters in close formation at the annual Farnborough Airshow. Nevertheless, the costs of forming display teams from very expensive and complex fighter aircraft, to say nothing of the consumption of precious aircraft fatigue, saw the demise of many individual fighter squadron teams in the early 1960s. The Red Arrows' predecessors were the Yellow Jacks, formed originally at Valley by flying instructors who had flown with the Black Arrows, flying Gnats painted bright yellow. The RAF needed a new team to replace the Black Arrows and the Lightning equipped Firebirds, but did not consider yellow to be a suitable colour for the aircraft of its official aerobatic display team. The team was reformed as an element of the Central Flying School and renamed the Red Arrows, with the Gnats being repainted bright red. By the end of the 1970s even the small teams at Flying Training Schools had virtually all disappeared leaving only the Red Arrows, who exchanged their Gnats for the Hawk in 1980. Individual front line and training RAF aircraft were still displayed at airshows, the pilots being drawn from individual units prepared to make the extra effort to provide them.

My first foray into the display world took place in 1985. At the time I was commanding 237 Operational Conversion Unit, equipped with the Buccaneer and a number of two seat Hunters, based at RAF Lossiemouth. I succeeded in persuading not only my Station Commander but also the air staff at our Group HQ to allow me to fly a limited number of displays in the Hunter, an aircraft much loved by the public but only used now by the Buccaneer squadrons as a trainer at Lossiemouth in the far north of Scotland, so rarely in the public eye. The Hunter T7 was not an ideal display aircraft, the visibility from the cockpit was rather limited when compared to the single seat aircraft so I often had a navigator with me in the right hand seat to provide lookout and to keep an eye on what I was doing. The T7 also had the less powerful version of the Avon engine so performance was limited and care was needed particularly in vertical manoeuvres, as was demonstrated sadly and at great cost many years later at Shoreham. I enjoyed displaying the Hunter and found the experience very valuable, ignorant at that time of what lay ahead in the future.

My next appointment was to the Central Flying School (CFS) at RAF Scampton as Officer Commanding Examining Wing, generally known throughout the RAF as the Chief Trapper. Examining Wing's role was to carry out upgrade tests on Qualified Flying Instructors and to check overall flying standards throughout the three Services on behalf of the Commandant CFS, and to undertake similar visits overseas on the invitation of foreign air forces. A previous OC Examining Wing once described the role to me as being 'the aviation equivalent of having a licence to print money.' During the two years and six months of this tour I qualified as first pilot in no fewer than 22 different types so my predecessor was absolutely correct in his description. The CFS had originally been based at RAF Little Rissington in Glouctershire, with a satellite airfield just down the road at Kemble used by the Red Arrows and the CFS Gnat squadron.

In 1976 Little Rissington was closed; the Red Arrows remained at Kemble, the Gnat squadron moved to Valley and the rest of CFS was sent to Cranwell, so CFS really wasn't Central any more. Then another move took place with the Cranwell based element of CFS moving to Leeming in Yorkshire, putting the supervisory staff and Commandant even further away from the Red Arrows, who lived a life of unsupervised luxury at Kemble. This situation was remedied in 1984 when the last Vulcan squadrons were disbanded, leaving the large and well-founded airfield at Scampton vacant. CFS moved in from Leeming and the Red Arrows were evicted from their comfortable unsupervised existence at Kemble to rejoin CFS at Scampton, where they had to live under the direct gaze of the Commandant CFS and his staff (plate31). Thus CFS recovered a degree of its original centralization, although its helicopter and Hawk elements remained at Shawbury and Valley respectively. This was the situation that I found on arrival in 1987.

The Hawk had now been in service as an advanced trainer at Valley for over 10 years, where it had replaced the Gnat, and also as a tactics and weapons lead-in trainer at Chivenor and Brawdy, replacing the Hunter. As an advanced trainer it was a vast improvement on the Gnat. The view from the rear seat was excellent, the built-in gas turbine starter meant it could operate away from home base without ground support, it had an outstanding turning performance and considerable range; after climbing to 40,000ft it could travel some 1000 nm. Although not as fast as the Gnat, a clean aircraft could be persuaded just to exceed Mach1 in a very steep dive. It was reliable and handled superbly. In the tactics and weapon training role it was equipped with a gun sight and three weapons hard points. The centre line hard point carried a podded 30mm cannon, the wing hard points could carry practice bomb carriers, rocket pods or AIM 9 Sidewinder missiles. Equipped with 2 Sidewinder air-to-air missiles and the cannon it replaced the Hunter in the short-range air defence role. It even had a baggage container into which two people could stow a reasonable amount of clothing, a feature completely absent in the Gnat. The Hawks used by the Red Arrows (plate 30) carried a pod on the centre line hard point filled with diesel and coloured dye for smoke generation; the engine was also modified to give a more rapid response to throttle movement, necessary for accurate aerobatic close formation flying.

One of the more interesting tasks that fell to Examining Wing was to check out the flying skills of the Red Arrows' pilots just before the Team left for its final work up in Cyprus, where they would be given their approval to display in front of the public by the Air Officer Commanding Support Command. At the end of the previous season up to three pilots would leave, to be replaced by the new boys who spent the winter months working hard to acquire the close formation aerobatic flying skills needed. By March the Team would start flying as a nine aircraft formation for the first time and this was normally when Examining Wing would arrive to carry out their checks. Two of us, usually my fast jet examiner and I, would spend a whole week flying with the Team. We would fly individual handling sorties with every pilot, usually a mixture of general handling, practice emergency procedures and instrument flying, each flight lasting about an hour. Unsurprisingly, given the nature of their winter work up flying, some of the pilot's instrument flying skills proved a bit rusty.

Then we would fly with every pilot during formation aerobatic practices, not to assess on their skill in formation flying but to present them with unexpected simulated emergencies, such as an engine fire in the middle of a nine aircraft formation loop or barrel roll. This could be quite exciting as our victim tried safely to break out of the formation, deal correctly with the problem and bring the exercise to a successful conclusion, which might even have been simulating abandoning the aircraft. At the end of the week a report on every pilot's performance would be raised, forming an important element in the ultimate confirmation of the Team's suitability to display in public. During the subsequent display season occasionally there would be an opportunity to see that all was going well on the Team and the sortie chosen for this chapter heading was one of these. The event was fairly low key, an in-season practice at RAF Marham, coinciding with the station's Family's Day. There would have been no opportunity for me in the back seat to get any 'hands on' time but it was intriguing to witness a full display routine from one of the participating aircraft, in this case Red 9. To see another aircraft approaching you head on, at a closing speed of nearly 800kts, was somewhat unnerving.

Every year CFS hosted and judged the Wright Jubilee Trophy aerobatic competition, when the Flying Training Schools sent their individual display pilots to compete for idividual trophies and being chosen as the Command display pilot for their aircraft type in the forthcoming summer display season. The aircraft types were Bulldog, Gazelle, Tucano, Jet Provost and Hawk. Judging this competition was interesting work. One year we invited Brian Lecomber, a noted aerobatic champion more used to performing extreme aerobatics in a highly manoeuvrable specialist aircraft, to join our team of judges. He found it very strange that the RAF's repertoire of aerobatics was so pedestrian when compared to what he was used to. Thus by the end of my time at CFS in 1990 I had a reasonable grasp of the challenges and pitfalls of display flying, having not only recently displayed the Hunter but also having been involved in the checking and supervision of Red Arrows display flying and judging the Wright Jubilee competition.

A staff appointment followed my time at CFS, then a couple of years commanding RAF Linton on Ouse, during which the station provided the Bulldog, Jet Provost and Tucano display pilots for the summer air displays. Moving on a few years, in 2003 I was a full time reservist on Cambridge University Air Squadron. One day I was invited by my long-standing friend and colleague Rick Peacock-Edwards to join the Flying Control Committee (FCC) at the Imperial War Museum Duxford (plate 32). This voluntary task proved to be both challenging and enjoyable. The role of the FCC is to ensure that display pilots adhere to the regulations governing air displays issued by the Civilian Aviation Authority (CAA), to monitor the conduct of the air display and to take the appropriate action if a potentially dangerous situation develops. One of my first air displays at Duxford proved to be a baptism of fire. During the 2003 Flying Legends Air Show a Fairey Firefly aircraft operated by the Royal Navy Historic Flight carried out a manoeuvre that was doomed to fail and the aircraft crashed, killing both occupants.

As I had witnessed the event from the top of the control tower I found myself as a witness at the RN Board of Inquiry, whose members had all been students of mine at various stages in the past. After giving my formal evidence, the President described, off the record, how through a series of unconnected events a pilot who really did not have the right background or experience found himself flying a 1940s vintage aircraft in the challenging air display business, where there is no room for error. Thankfully no spectators were involved. A further sadness for me was that the Firefly had been obtained by HMS Victorious way back in 1966 from Australia, when I was serving on board. It had been presented to the Fleet Air Arm Museum when Victorious arrived back at Portsmouth in 1967, then identified as suitable for restoration to flying condition. In 2003 it had only just emerged from a long period of restoration work undertaken by apprentices at BAe's factory at Brough.

In addition to being a member of the Duxford FCC I found myself being asked to be a member of the FCC at minor displays at Blenheim Palace, Cambridge and Bristol, and also to undertake the role of Flying Display Director (FDD) at Whitehaven, Seething and Old Buckenham. The FDD's task was altogether more complex and demanding when compared to being a member of the FCC. The FDD had to devise a flying programme for the day, ensure that every participant's insurance and display currency was up to date and correct, to make sure that the permission to hold a display had been obtained from the CAA in time and to produce suitable briefing material for the event. On the day itself the FDD is required to brief all participants face to face or by phone, and to actively manage the conduct of the event with the assistance of the FCC. Legal responsibility for the conduct of the event now became an issue which, at the time of writing (2017), is still very much open to debate following the accident at the Shoreham display in 2015, when 11 persons outside the display venue were killed when a Hunter crashed during the display. Some time before this disaster I decided to hand over any remaining commitments I had as a FDD because they were getting very time consuming; in hindsight this seems to have been a prudent move. In summary, the conduct and management of air displays is now rightly vastly more complex than in the 1940s, when the Station Commander could take part in an air race on Battle of Britain Day with no previous training or experience.

CHAPTER FIFTEEN

COMMANDANT AND AIR OFFICER COMMANDING

LOGBOOK ENTRY, HARRY EELES

17 May 1954
Balliol WG118
Self/ Flt Lt MacCorkindale
To & from Oakington
1 hour

We moved from France to Cranwell in September 1952, arriving there on my 10th birthday. Much to my displeasure not a great deal of notice was taken of this event as my parents plunged immediately into the whirlwind of life as Commandant and Air Officer Commanding of the RAF College (plate 33). Within minutes of our arrival the official guests for that weekend, the aged Bishop of Litchfield and his wife, also arrived requiring VIP treatment. The Bishop was due to preach at the Cranwell church that Sunday. The church was a converted aircraft hangar dating from the days of the First World War and the protocol for arrival there for morning service had to be followed precisely. My sister, brother and I were horrified to discover we had to walk in at the very last moment, in front of all the assembled congregation of officers and their wives and the Flight Cadets, whose attendance was mandatory rather than optional.

We had to sit right at the front in their full view, so no chance of reading a smuggled in comic. This was quite a shock to the system. Living in The Lodge must have been similar in many ways to Harry Eeles's childhood days in Wavendon House, except this time it was his children rather than him who were living behind the green baize door. There were numerous staff to assist the running of The Lodge, a full time gardener, a senior batman with other part time helpers, a service driver and a cook. The Lodge was full of valuable paintings, including a Gainsborough, which had been left on loan by a wealthy Lincolnshire family until the heir apparent came of age. Any damage to them caused by children's play would have resulted in very serious punishment for the offender, hence our incarceration behind the green baize door.

Cranwell was a busy, exciting place in the 1950s. Both north and south airfields were still without hard runways but in constant use. Flying training to wings standard was carried out on the Percival Prentice and the Harvard. The Prentice was an ugly, ungainly looking trainer, which was soon replaced by the elegant Chipmunk. The noisy Harvard also disappeared not long after our arrival, to be replaced in turn by the Boulton Paul Balliol. The Balliol was a strange choice of trainer for the RAF, being something of an anachronism when it entered RAF service. The front line aircraft of both Fighter Command (Venom, Meteor, Hunter, Javelin) and Bomber Command (Canberra, Valiant, Vulcan, Victor) in the mid '50s were changing steadily to become virtually all jet powered, leaving only Transport Command (Hastings, Beverley) and Coastal Command (Shackleton) as the principle piston engine operators, but even for these the end of the piston engine era was not far off.

The Balliol (plates 34, 35) was similar in many ways to a fighter of the Second World War. It was designed to meet Specification T7/45, which called for an all-purpose trainer to be fitted with a turboprop, but this configuration never proved satisfactory. A Merlin 35 piston engine powered the T2 version of the Balliol, it had a tail wheel undercarriage and featured side-by-side seating. It bore no resemblance in appearance, performance or handling to the front line aircraft of the period such as the Meteor, Venom, Vampire and Canberra. However, it was well suited to operating from the grass surface of the south airfield at Cranwell as well as the hard runways at Barkston Heath, Cranwell's satellite airfield. It would bite if handled incorrectly and it suffered particularly from a phenomenon known as 'torque stall'. Torque stall occurred when a large power demand was made at low speed; the torque effect of the Merlin could overcome the balancing aerodynamic forces and roll the aircraft rapidly onto its back. As this was most likely to happen on a baulked approach close to the ground the result was usually fatal, not a good characteristic for a training aircraft. No Balliol has survived today in an airworthy condition; if one had it would have been invaluable as a trainer for today's warbird pilots. There were also a couple of Meteor T7s based at Cranwell to give a bit of jet experience to the cadets before they moved on to their next phase of training on jet aircraft.

This logbook entry reveals that the Commandant was provided with an ADC to assist with his busy schedule in exactly the same way that he had done back in 1933 in Egypt. As in 1933, the ADC's name appears often in my father's logbook, but I suspect rather more as a passenger than pilot in command. Flight Lieutenant Peter McCorkindale was a very smart young officer and he and his wife soon became firm family friends. My father was asked to be godfather to his son Simon, who eventually followed a successful career as a film star. Flying the Merlin powered Balliol would have presented no problem to Harry Eeles, whose flying experience was still predominantly in piston-engined aircraft, but the Balliol's time in RAF service was not to last long.

A former Flight Cadet from my father's time as Commandant, now retired Group Captain Nigel Walpole, flew the Balliol during his time at Cranwell. He describes vividly what it was like to fly. *'Following 126 hours flying in 1953, on the innocuous Chipmunk (see Chapter 2), I flew 56 hours on the T6 Harvard in the first three months of 1954, followed by 112 hours on the Balliol T2 in two terms, Mar – Dec 1954 – then on to Meteors. The venerable Harvard was simple and a pure delight to fly. With its 600 hp Pratt and Whitney Wasp radial engine, it had a top speed of about 200 mph, and a max height of 20,000ft. I remember no vices other than a tendency to 'ground loop' if you relaxed on the landing roll, and I particularly liked the tandem seating – good preparation for single seat fighters! I found the Balliol T2, with its 1245hp Rolls Royce Merlin 35 V 12 piston engine equally splendid in many ways, although the huge 'fan' at the front had a great deal of torque, compared with the Harvard. Accordingly, we had to work hard to maintain balanced flight, with judicious use of the rudder and rudder trim, and no matter how many warnings we were given, some still managed to induce a potentially lethal 'torque stall', typically with too rapid a throttle movement on an overshoot. I saw two Balliols upside down at Barkston Heath, Cranwell's satellite airfield. I found no difficulty coping with the increased speeds on take-off and landing, and it was wonderful to have so much power for aerobatics (and illegal air combat). However, the torque again made the already complicated 'Pattern G'(or was it 'Pattern H ?') more difficult in our Instrument Rating Tests, 'under the hood'.*

If I recall correctly, these patterns had four legs, each to be flown at different speeds and heights, and ending with a 270 degree climbing or descending turn, again at specified speeds, on to the next leg – always watching that swinging ball on the turn and slip indicator. There was a very worrying accident rate, mainly (but not all!) due to technical defects, especially with the Merlin engine – allegedly built by Packard. One of my Entry had an engine failure during his Final Handling Test, and executed a fine forced landing in a cornfield – with his instructor looking on. It seemed rather unkind to re-schedule the test, simply because one minor drill had not been completed. The Balliol had two small stubs appearing through the top skin of the inner mainplane when the landing gear was down and locked – confirming the 'two greens' in the cockpit, but I found that even this double check was not infallible. Having called 'Finals, two greens and visual indicators' on runway 27 at Barkston, I landed smoothly (I was well known for it!) only to have my port leg fold up and send me careering over to the dispersal – between two petrol bowsers. With so many other accidents to deal with, OC Flying, Wing Commander McDougal was frantic, so I was pleased to hear, that evening, that a fault had been replicated on jacks in the hangar – and I was exonerated. I understand that it may have been the excessive accident rate that led to the withdrawal of the Balliol after only two years service at Cranwell, and I believe it only served the RAF as an advanced trainer at one other station, RAF Cottesmore. I loved the Balliol – but not the side-by-side seating.'

In 1954 the grass south airfield at Cranwell was finally given two hard runways, associated taxiways and hard standings, ushering in jet training aircraft in the shape of the Vampire T11, but not before my father had carried out the first landing on the new runway in an Anson. At the same time the Piston Provost, a more powerful and robust trainer, replaced the Chipmunk. Thus when his tour at Cranwell finished in 1956, Harry Eeles had overseen considerable changes to the way in which the RAF College undertook its business. He was awarded the CB for his work as Commandant and, aged only 46, it seemed he had much still to look forward to in his RAF career. He was disappointed with his next appointment, Director of Administrative Plans in the Air Ministry, without promotion. After the Defence White Paper of 1957, when Secretary of State for Defense Duncan Sandys forecast the early demise of the manned combat aircraft in favour of guided missiles, he was informed somewhat impersonally that his services were no longer required as a consequence of a redundancy programme within the RAF. In many ways this was a sad end to what had so far been a distinguished career. He retired to live in his home in Wiltshire and died in 1992 aged 82.

Many years later, when visiting his ADC from Cranwell days, by now also retired as a Group Captain, I asked if he had any idea why my father's RAF career had come to rather an abrupt end. Peter McCorkindale agreed that it was an unexpected conclusion, but offered the view that there were two things that had contributed to this. One was the high accident rate at Cranwell in the mid- 1950s. By this time, with the country not engaged in major hostilities, the Government in particular wished to see fewer costly accidents. My father, brought up in an era when flying accidents were everyday occurrences, perhaps never quite grasped the importance of the need for greater safety in the air. Secondly, he brought in many changes to the Cranwell system of training which, whilst popular at Cranwell, did not always meet the universal approval of some ex Flight Cadet senior RAF officers who had graduated many years previously and were now in positions of high command and influence. Nevertheless, Harry Eeles always remembered his time as Commandant at the RAF College as the best experience of his career; he still holds the record of being the longest serving Commandant.

CHAPTER SIXTEEN

STATION COMMANDER

LOGBOOK ENTRY, TOM EELES

16 September 1993
Jet Provost T5A XW 359
Self
Staff Continuation Training, last Jet Provost flight,
50 minutes, 10 minutes actual Instrument Flying, 1 Precision
Radar Approach

I was fortunate enough to gain wide experience as a flying instructor in the RAF, ranging from the elementary phase on a University Air Squadron (Bulldog, Tutor) through basic (JP, Tucano), advanced (Gnat, Hawk), multi engine (Jetstream) to Tactical Weapons and OCU (Hunter, Buccaneer) and CFS (Examining Wing). Way back over half a century ago, when I first started flying training as a pilot at the RAF College Cranwell, the RAF could proudly claim that it led the world with its system of 'all through jet' basic flying training for pilots. The Jet Provost, known always as the JP, had replaced the old piston engine basic trainers, such as the Prentice, Provost and Chipmunk. Student pilots started on the Mk3 version then moved on to fly the more powerful Mk4, completing a course of 180 hours for Cranwell students and somewhat less for direct entry pilots who spent less time in training. There was then a split; pilots destined for fighters and bombers moved on to fly the Vampire T11, which was replaced by the Gnat T1 in 1963. Those selected for transports and maritime patrol aircraft flew the Varsity, which in turn was replaced by the Jetstream in the early 1970s.

There was no grading or elementary flying training phase in this system, candidates being selected for pilot training solely on their aptitude scores achieved in initial recruitment. When first tour pilots began to be selected for the Lightning an additional pre OCU course in basic tactical flying and weapon delivery on the Hunter was added to improve a student's chances of graduating on a more complex combat aircraft where flying hours were more expensive; with the introduction in the late 1960s of the Phantom, Buccaneer, Harrier, Jaguar and later the Tornado this course was included for all future pilots of these types. This system worked well but was not without its problems. The Jet Provost was considered by many to be too easy to fly, allowing individuals of limited ability to progress on to the more expensive and difficult Gnat, with the consequent risk of failure. The Gnat, a lovely aircraft when it was serviceable, was short-legged and complex, earning the reputation of being an airborne emergencies trainer that could not venture far from the North Wales Area of Intensive Aerial Activity. The Hawk, a much more capable and reliable aircraft, replaced the Gnat in 1978. In the 1960s there was only a limited ab initio rotary option. Failure in either the fast jet or multi streams would usually end up as navigators. The expansion of the RAF's support helicopter force saw the introduction of more rotary courses, with students leaving the Jet Provost syllabus about a third of the way through to move direct to rotary training.

Then in the 1980s a Flying Selection Squadron equipped with the ubiquitous Chipmunk was established as an experiment, to see if a short course of elementary flying training on a cheap, simple aircraft could weed out those of low ability before they started flying more expensive and complex aircraft. At about the same time a study by CFS concluded that a basic trainer that would be more fuel efficient but with more demanding handling characteristics should replace the Jet Provost; the consequent competition resulted in the turbo prop Tucano being selected, which was claimed to have 'jet like handling' despite its large propeller and turbo prop engine. Thus the original concept of an 'all through jet basic flying training' syllabus came to an end.

In 1992 I was appointed as Station Commander of RAF Linton on Ouse (plate 36), home base of No 1 Flying Training School (FTS), the Royal Navy Elementary Flying Training Squadron (RNEFTS) and RAF Bulldog Standards Squadron. This was as close as I ever got to my father's five stints as a Station Commander at the Fighter Command airfields of Drem, Ayr, Catterick, Colerne and Thorney Island, and his time as Commandant and Air Officer Commanding RAF College Cranwell, but the opportunities for command appointments of this nature were few and far between in the 1990s when compared to the 1940s and 50s. The RAF was very much smaller now. Sadly, by now my father was in terminal decline with dementia; I do not think he ever realized I was now a Station Commander of an extensive parish of a main airfield and three subsidiary relief landing grounds; he passed away in June 1992, just after his eighty-second birthday. Nevertheless, despite its lower status when compared to Cranwell, Linton was a very busy and exciting station to command. Additionally there were 3 relief landing grounds at Church Fenton, Dishforth and Topcliffe to look after, the old airfield at Elvington to dispose of and many civic commitments in the city of York, where Linton had been granted Freedom of the City, to keep us busy. It was a particular delight to renew my acquaintance with the Royal Navy in the form of the RNEFTS, especially as the senior naval officer at Linton, Commander Barry Kirby, had served with me on HMS Victorious many years previously.

In 1992 No1 FTS was the last FTS training pilots to remain equipped with the long-serving Jet Provost in its T3A and T5A (plate 37) versions, the only other basic FTS at Cranwell having been re-equipped with the Tucano. Thus for a while we were still doing 'all through jet basic flying training' that I had started on some 30 years previously, but not for long. I collected the first Tucano destined for 1 FTS from Church Fenton on 3rd April 1992, having already flown the Tucano during my tour with CFS Examining Wing. It was not long before we had a sizeable fleet of Tucanos at Linton but the Jet Provost lingered on for eighteen more months, mainly to provide refresher flying for student pilots who were holding whilst waiting for further training courses. During the build up to the first Gulf War and its active phase the multi engine Operational Conversion Units stopped training in order to bolster the needs of the large airlift task; this had a major effect on the training pipeline leaving those students selected for multi engine flying stuck with nowhere to go.

Finally, by mid 1993 this backlog started to clear and the need to retain the Jet Provost disappeared. A number were flown into the grass airfield at Halton to be used for apprentice engineer training, others were delivered to the storage unit at RAF Shawbury for subsequent sale to private owners. Eventually one solitary JP 3A remained in a corner of a hangar awaiting collection by a private owner once his cheque had been cleared. The explosive devices in the ejection seats had been removed as a condition of sale but the seats and parachutes remained installed, with the redundant later leg restraint cords neatly coiled under the seats so that the seats could be properly fixed in position with their top latches engaged. The proud new owner collected his JP but shortly afterwards at some point took out the right hand seat, disturbing the neatly coiled leg restraint cords, which he presumed were done that way as part of RAF bull. When the seat was put back its top latch was not properly engaged because of the tangle of leg restraint cords under the seat. Some time later the proud owner offered his brother a trip in the JP. Whilst strapping in the brother failed to connect two vital straps, which ensured that the parachute did not slide up his body when deployed, as he was told that they were part of the inhibited ejection seat and were therefore redundant. So the stage is now set for disaster; our hero is strapped incorrectly into a seat that is not properly secured to the aircraft.

Once airborne and at a safe altitude our hero is offered some aerobatics which included a slow roll. As the JP became inverted the proud owner was astonished by the sudden departure of his brother in his seat through the aircraft's canopy. On finding himself suddenly falling through space our hero had the presence of mind to pull the parachute rip cord. However, the seat was still connected to the parachute assembly. The parachute deploys and because those vital straps are undone the harness, with seat connected, slides up our hero's body, leaving him suspended by the neck and arms and in serious danger of being strangled. Luck was on his side that day as he arrived on terra firma before further damage occurred and he lived to tell the tale.

What was the Jet Provost like to fly? The JP3 was very docile and somewhat under-powered, being known to many as 'the constant thrust, variable noise' machine. It was ideal for the early stages of flying training but most students soon grew out of it and needed something with more performance to stretch their ability. It was followed quickly into service by the JP4, an identical airframe but with a more powerful engine. This became a popular aircraft for advanced aerobatics and was capable of reaching significant altitudes. Since it was unpressurised this resulted in many pilots suffering from a variety of the symptoms of decompression sickness so the JP5 appeared. This version retained the same engine as the JP4 but had a new front fuselage section with a completely different profile and incorporating a pressurised cockpit. It was soon discovered that the JP5 had some rather unpleasant spinning characteristics, particularly if flown solo and fitted with wing tip tanks. Strakes were fitted to the forward fuselage, roughened leading edges were put on the outer wings and tip tanks were not fitted to JP5s used by FTSs carrying out pilot flying training where many sorties were flown by solo students. In this configuration the JP5 proved to be an excellent and popular trainer. The JP4 soon disappeared from the scene, mainly worn out by extensive aerobatics, leaving only the JP 3 and 5 in the training fleet. A modest avionic upgrade incorporating VOR/DME and ILS produced the 3A and 5A. The JP also earned considerable export sales as the Strikemaster, which could carry an effective armament used in the ground attack role.

As the end of the JP's service drew near I felt some commemoration should be made of its outstanding record of service. We held a special event at Linton on Ouse with a short flying display, which included solo aerobatics by a JP and a mass flypast of a formation in the shape of the letters JP. A formal Guest Night was held that night in the Officers' Mess and the flypast was recorded in an oil painting done by a local artist who kindly presented it to the Station. One of the oldest JP3s was selected to be the Gate Guardian to mark the long association of Linton on Ouse with the JP. Whilst it was being prepared for positioning near the Station entrance by Airwork, who held the contract to provide aircraft servicing, Mr Terry Stone the Airwork manager suggested that a plaque giving the aircraft's history should be positioned by it. I noted that the JP had served at Cranwell in the early 1960s and observed that I might even have flown it then. Careful perusal of the JP's Form 700 revealed my signature; the first time I had flown it was my first jet solo on 2nd February 1962, an extraordinary coincidence. And so we said farewell to the trusty JP. I flew my last trip in it on 16 September 1993, on my own. I did some aerobatics, some low flying, an instrument approach and a few circuits. The first 'all through jet basic trainer' passed into history, although some still survive to fly in civilian ownership.

CHAPTER SEVENTEEN

THE LAST LOGBOOK ENTRIES

HARRY EELES
29 Nov 1957
Anson 531
Flt Lt Rowell/Self
Feltwell – Old Sarum
1 hour

TOM EELES
25 Jun 2010
Tutor G BYWS
Flt Lt Rawnsley/Self
Low Level nav, general handling
1 hour 40 min

After his time as Commandant at Cranwell Harry Eeles was posted to the Air Ministry as Director of Administrative Plans, hardly a good reward for four years in a very demanding and high profile appointment that would appear to have been very successful. I suspect that the lack of promotion must have been a great disappointment. It would seem that many of the necessary changes he introduced at the RAF College did not always meet with universal approval from the higher echelons of the service, particularly from those well versed with the older ways of life at Cranwell. The issue of high loss rates in flying training was a matter that must have had some bearing in this. We lived between two homes, a large rented flat in Kensington and the family home in Wiltshire where most of the holidays were spent. I really have no idea what the Director of Admin Plans's work involved, all I can remember is that there was a steady supply of aeronautical magazines that came my way from his office.

I was intent on pursuing a career as an RAF pilot and after attending the selection board at RAF Hornchurch and Daedalus House at Cranwell was awarded a sixth form scholarship that guaranteed entry to Cranwell provided I obtained the necessary two A level passes. There are two short refresher courses in late 1956 and 1957 recorded in my father's logbook, flying the Meteor T7 at the School of Refresher Flying at RAF Manby. He undertook a further refresher course on the Piston Provost at RAF Feltwell in November 1957. At the end of the month, after a mere 18 hours flying which included an Instrument Rating Test, he flew in a trusty Anson (plate 38), a type he first flew in 1939, from Feltwell to Old Sarum, the nearest airfield to our Wiltshire home. This proved to be his last recorded flight in an RAF aircraft. By now the ramifications of Duncan Sandys's 1957 Defence White Paper were beginning to become apparent. It had optimistically predicted the imminent end of the need for manned combat aircraft, which were to be replaced entirely by guided missiles. This aspiration far outstretched the available technology of the time but would result in a dramatic reduction in the number of pilots needed in the RAF, the consequent prospect of reduced defence costs being doubtless most attractive to politicians. Inevitably a redundancy scheme was introduced and a very curt and formal letter informed my father that his services as an RAF officer were no longer required. He left the RAF in early 1958 after a distinguished career that ended in a way that he had probably not expected.

I, on the other hand, was considerably luckier. After my time at Linton on Ouse I found myself working in the Defence Exports Services Organisation in London, my one and only foray into the Ministry of Defence. The great advantage of this appointment was that it allowed me to escape from London around midday most Fridays. I would take the train to Cambridge and then fly Air Training Corps cadets on air experience flights with 5 Air

Experience Flight (AEF) in the evergreen Chipmunk at Cambridge Airport, alongside the Bulldogs of Cambridge University Air Squadron (CUAS). When the mandatory retirement age of 55 arrived in 1997 I applied for and got the job of flying instructor on CUAS in the full time reservist rank of Flight Lieutenant, flying the Bulldog. Money spent on a new uniform was reduced by the simple measure of cutting my Group Captain's rank tabs in half. There followed seven very happy and busy years on CUAS. In 1999 the Grob 115E Tutor replaced the Bulldog and the squadron moved from Cambridge to RAF Wyton, an unpopular move for the students and myself.

For me, the Tutor (plate 39) was a bit of a disappointment after the Bulldog. It was constructed of glass reinforced plastic and powered by a Lycoming air cooled engine driving a wooden three blade constant speed propellor. It was provided by a contractor and was on the civilian register, therefore had to be flown in accordance with the civil Air Navigation Order (ANO) rather than military flying regulations. In many areas the ANO was more restrictive than military flying regulations. The Tutor had lower cross wind operating limits than the Bulldog and could be quite a handful in strong crosswinds. Initially it was not cleared to fly in cloud and many of our normal aerobatic manoeuvres were not permitted despite the aircraft being well capable of performing them. Eventually these problems were resolved.

The next drama occurred when the propeller of a Tutor failed in flight and shed its blades. The aircraft was forced to land in a field and a long period of inactivity followed. The view from the cockpit was poor in the critical area ahead at the 10 o'clock and 2 o'clock sectors, caused by a very wide canopy/windscreen frame.This undoubtedly contributed to a fatal mid air collision in which four aircrew died. After seven very busy years both at work and play with CUAS the RAF decided not to renew the contracts of many reservists on university air squadrons as there was a surplus of RAF pilots who needed experience as QFIs. Undeterred, I cut my rank tabs in half again, was commissioned as a Flying Officer in the RAF Volunteer Reserve and moved across the hangar to continue Tutor flying with 5 AEF. I continued to enjoy another six years of most enjoyable flying until 2010, when the fallout from a fatal accident at another AEF resulted in a ban on all those over the age of 65 from flying as captain in a service operated aircraft, regardless of their medical fitness.

Quite suddenly and without warning I was grounded, just short of achieving 8500 military flying hours, an achievement I had already decided would mark my retirement. My AEF Flight Commander, Squadron Leader Stu Rawnsley, very kindly offered to let me have a few more sorties with a younger man in order to get to 8500 hours. My final flight on 25 June 2010 was with Stu Rawnsley, a very pleasant low level navigation trip around East Anglia, during which we passed close to Feltwell where my father had flown for the last time 53 years previously, followed by some aerobatics and a few circuits to clock up the needed flying time. After landing a celebratory glass or two of champagne (plate 40) were consumed to mark the end of what had been a most enjoyable 50 years of flying in my father's slipstream.

ANNEX A

THE AIRCRAFT – A COMPARISON

HARRY EELES

Avro 504N
 Engine – Lynx
 Span – 36ft
 Max speed – 100mph
 Role – flying training

Bristol Bulldog
 Engine – Bristol Jupiter 440hp
 Span – 33ft
 Max speed – 178mph
 Role – day/night fighter

Fairey IIIF
 Engine – Napier Lion
 Span – 45ft
 Max speed – 120mph
 Role – general purposes/light transport

Hawker Hart
 Engine – Rolls Royce Kestrel
 Span – 37ft
 Max speed – 185mph
 Role – light bomber/flying training

Westland Whirlwind F1
 Engines – 2 Rolls Royce Peregrine 880hp
 Span – 45ft
 Max speed – 400mph(diving)
 Role – day fighter/ground attack

Beechcraft C45
 Engines – Pratt and Whitney Wasp Junior 450hp
 Span – 47ft
 Max speed – 195kts
 Role – light transport/training

TOM EELES

De Havilland Chipmunk T10
 Engine – Gypsy Major 145 HP
 Span – 34ft
 Max speed – 173kts
 Role – flying training

English Electric Canberra B(I)8
 Engines – 2 Rolls Royce Avon turbo-jets
 Span – 63ft
 Max speed – 450 kts/M0.84
 Role – light bomber/ground attack

Blackburn Buccaneer S2
 Engines – 2 Rolls Royce Spey turbo-fans
 Span – 44ft
 Max speed – 580kts/M0.95
 Role – maritime strike/attack

Folland Gnat T1
 Engine – Bristol Siddeley Orpheus turbo-jet
 Span – 24ft
 Max speed – 0.9M/500kts
 Role – flying training

Hawker Hunter FG(A)9
 Engine – Rolls Royce Avon turbo-jet
 Span – 33ft
 Max speed – 620kts/no Mach limit
 Role – day fighter/ground attack

Jetstream T1
 Engines – Turbomeca Astazou turbo prop
 Span – 52ft
 Max speed – 245kts
 Role - light transport/training

De Havilland Vampire F1
  Engine – De Havilland Goblin turbo jet
  Span – 38ft
  Max speed – 520mph
  Role – day fighter

Boulton Paul Balliol T2
  Engine – Rolls Royce Merlin
  Span – 39ft
  Max speed – 288mph
  Role – flying training

Avro Anson
  Engines – 2 Armstrong Siddeley Cheetah 420hp
  Span – 57ft
  Max speed – 170mph
  Role – light transport

BAe Hawk T1
  Engine – Rolls Royce Adour turbo-fan
  Span – 30ft
  Max speed – 550kt/1.01M
  Role – flying training/display flying

BAe Jet Provost T5A
  Engine – Rolls Royce Viper turbo-jet
  Span – 35ft
  Max speed – 400kts
  Role – flying training

Grob G115E Tutor
  Engine – Lycoming 160hp
  Span – 32ft
  Max speed – 185kt
  Role – flying training

ANNEX B

RECORD OF SERVICE

Air Commodore Harry Eeles

1929-30 RAF College, Cranwell, officer and flying training.
1930-32 41 Squadron, RAF Northolt, squadron pilot.
1932-34 ADC to AOC RAF Middle East, HQ MEAF
1934-35 Air Armament School course.
1935-37 5FTS, flying instructor.
1937-40 Personal Assistant to Chief of Air Staff, Air Ministry.
1940 263 Squadron, Commanding Officer
1941 RAF Drem, Commanding Officer
1941 RAF Ayr, Commanding Officer
1942 RAF Catterick, Commanding Officer
1942-43 RAF Colerne, Commanding Officer
1944 HQ Fighter Command, Air Staff.
1944-45 HQ 85 Group, 2nd Tactical Air Force, Air Staff
1945 HQ Fighter Command, Air Staff
1946-48 RAF Delegation, United Nations, New York
1948-50 RAF Thorney Island, Commanding Officer
1950 School of Land/Air Warfare, Air Staff
1951-52 Supreme HQ Allied Powers Europe, Air Staff
1952-56 AOC and Commandant, RAF College Cranwell
1956-58 Air Ministry, Director of Admin Plans

Group Captain Tom Eeles

1960-63 RAF College Cranwell, officer and flying training
1963-64 4 FTS RAF Valley, advanced flying training
1964 231 OCU, operational conversion course
1964-66 16 Squadron RAF Laarbruch, squadron pilot
1966-68 801 Naval Air Squadron, HMS Victorious, squadron pilot
1968 Central Flying School, flying instructor course.
1969 4 FTS RAF Valley, flying instructor
1969-70 736 Naval Air Squadron, flying instructor
1971-72 237 OCU, flying instructor
1972-75 12 Squadron, squadron pilot
1975-77 79 Squadron, Flight Commander
1977-79 237 OCU, Chief Flying Instructor
1980 Student, RAF Staff College
1981-82 Personal Staff Officer to Deputy C in C, RAF Strike Command
1982-84 HQ Air Support Command, Air Staff
1984-87 237 OCU, Officer Commanding
1987-89 Officer Commanding Examining Wing, Central Flying School
1990-92 HQ Air Support Command. Air Staff
1992-94 Station Commander, RAF Linton on Ouse
1995-97 Assistant Military Deputy (Air), DESO, MoD
1997-2004 Chief Flying Instructor, Cambridge University Air Squadron
2004-10 5 Air Experience Flight, squadron pilot

GLOSSARY OF TERMS

ADC	Aide de Camp
ATC	Air Traffic Control
BA	Bachelor of Arts
B(I)8	Bomber (Interdictor) 8, a version of the Canberra aircraft
C in C	Commander in Chief
CFS	Central Flying School
DESO	Defence Exports Services Organisation
DH	De Havilland, an aircraft manufacturer
DME	Distance Measuring Equipment
FEAF	Far East Air Force
FTS	Flying Training School
ILS	Instrument Landing System
IRBM	Intermediate Range Ballistic Missile
JP	Jet Provost training aircraft
KD	Khaki Drill uniform
LABS	Low Altitude Bombing Sysatem
MoT	Ministry of Transport roadworthiness test
NAS	Naval Air Squadron
NATO	North Atlantic Treaty Organisation
NCO	Non Commissioned Officer
OC	Officer Commanding
OCU	Operational Conversion Unit
QFI	Qualified Flying Instructor
QRA	Quick Reaction Alert
RFC	Royal Flying Corps
SHAPE	Supreme Headquarters Allied Powers Europe
TACAN	Tactical Air Navigation system
TSR2	Tactical, Strike and Reconaissance 2, a cancelled combat aircraft project
VIP	Very Important Person
VOR	Very high frequency Omni Range navigation system

INDEX

A

Aden 47, 48, 50, 51, 77.

Airfields
Bahrain 35, 40.
Boscombe Down 20.
Brawdy 76, 77, 79, 80, 100.
Changi 34, 35.
Cranwell 9, 12, 15 – 28, 99, 105 – 118.
Dishforth 67, 71.
Drem 67, 71, 72, 73, 95.
Duxford 54, 102, 103.
Feltwell 117, 118, 120.
Gan 34, 35, 40.
Gibraltar 76, 78 – 80.
Grangemouth 67, 70 – 73.
Hendon 16, 29, 55.
Kemble 65, 99.
Kuantan 35 – 40.
Laarbruch 21, 33, 35, 37, 40, 41, 48.
Linton on Ouse 26, 102, 113, 114, 116, 118.
Little Rissington 59, 99.
Lossiemouth 48, 59, 61, 66, 80, 90, 98.
Marham 86, 90, 97, 101.
Masirah 40.
Northolt 16, 28, 29, 31, 38, 72.
Old Sarum 96, 117, 118.
Ramstein 86, 87, 89.
Reading 28, 30, 31.
Scampton 99.
Sealand 45, 53, 54, 55.
Tengah 34, 36.
Thorney Island 85, 91, 93 – 95, 113.
Valley 59, 61 – 66, 98 – 100.
Wyton 86, 87, 89, 90, 119.

Aircraft
Anson 84, 109, 117, 118.
Atlas 18, 55, 56.
Avro 504 13, 18, 25, 26.
Balliol 13, 105 – 109.
Beechcraft C45 82 – 84.
Beverley 20, 106.

Bristol Bulldog 28, 29, 31, 44, 55.
Bristol Fighter 18, 43.
Britannia 35, 40, 48.
Buccaneer 47 – 50, 52, 59, 60, 66, 67, 79, 80, 98, 99, 111, 112.
BAe Bulldog 101, 102, 111, 113, 119.
Canberra 21, 32, 33, 37 – 40, 49, 58, 60, 106.
Chipmunk 20 – 26, 61, 106, 107, 109, 111, 112, 118.
Fairey IIIF 42, 44, 45.
Gnat 58 – 66, 98 – 100, 111, 112.
Hart 53, 55 – 57.
Hawk 65, 80, 97 – 101, 111, 112.
Hunter 20, 32, 50, 51, 60, 61, 64, 66, 76 – 81, 97, 98, 100, 103, 106, 111, 112.
Hurricane 57, 68, 70 – 73, 76.
Jet Provost 25, 26, 61, 101, 102, 111 – 115.
Jetstream 86 –88, 90, 111.
Meteor 20, 21, 74, 91 – 93, 106, 107, 118.
Moth 18.
Sea Vixen 50, 51.
Siskin 18, 19, 28, 29, 31.
Tucano 101, 102, 111, 112 – 114.
Tutor (Avro) 55, 56.
Tutor (Grob) 111, 117, 119, 120.
Vampire 60, 61, 91, 93, 94, 106, 109, 111.
Wapiti 53.
Whirlwind 60, 67 – 76, 84.

Ayers, Flt Lt 25.
Atbara 42, 44, 45.

B
Bond, Francis 14 – 16.
Bond, Jim 14 – 16.
Bond, Peter 15.
Brampton, RAF 87.

C
Cairo 43.
Camm, Sir Sidney 76.
Canada 83, 84.
China Rock Range 32, 38, 39.

E
Ed Darmer 42, 44, 45.
Edwards Jones, Humphrey 95.
Eeles/Bond, Florence 13, 14.
Eeles, Henry 13.

Egypt 42 – 57, 72.

F
Fitzgerald, Jim, Lt RN 47, 50.
Fleming, Ian 14, 15.

G
Germany 21, 32 – 38, 55, 67, 68, 87, 89.

H
Harrow School 14 – 16.
Hermes, HMS 50, 51, 52, 59.

J
JARIC 87 – 90,

K
Khartoum 42, 44, 45.

M
Macfadyen, Flt Lt 13, 18.
Macfadyen, Air Marshal Sir Ian iv, 12
McCorkindale, Peter, Flt Lt 107, 110.

N
Newall, Air Chief Marshal Sir Cyril 42, 44, 45.
Norton, Janet 45, 72.

P
Petter, W E 60, 67, 68.
'Phantom Dive' 92.

S
Singapore 34 – 38, 48.
Sherborne School 20, 21.
Squadrons/Units, RAF & RN
 No 16 21, 33, 37, 48.
 No 41 28, 29, 42.
 No 79 76.
 No 263 67 – 74.
 No 736 59, 66.
 No 801 48, 49, 52.
 CUAS 119.
 No 5 AEF 118, 120.
 CFS 59, 66, 97 – 102, 111, 112, 114.
 Red Arrows 65, 97 – 100.

No 1 FTS 113, 114.
No 4 FTS 59.
No 5 FTS 53, 54, 56, 57.
Stirrup, Jock, Gp Capt 89.
Sudan 44, 45.
Suez Canal 43, 47, 50, 53, 58.

U
USA 14, 33, 58, 74, 82 – 84, 87, 91, 93, 94.

T
Tredrey, Frank, Gp Capt 12, 56.

V
Victorious, HMS 48, 51, 52, 59, 103, 113.
Vincent, Stanley, Sqn Ldr 12, 28 – 31.

W
Walker, Sir 'Gus', Air Marshal 27.
Walpole, Nigel, Gp Capt 12, 108.

Printed in July 2021
by Rotomail Italia S.p.A., Vignate (MI) - Italy